HOWARD ZINN & LOIS MOTTONEN
FISTFIGHT IN THE EQUALITY STATE

HOWARD ZINN & LOIS MOTTONEN FISTFIGHT IN THE EQUALITY STATE

BY RODGER McDANIEL WITH LOIS MOTTONEN

WORDSWORTH
CODY, WYOMING

ALSO BY RODGER MCDANIEL

Dying for Joe McCarthy's Sins:
The Suicide of Wyoming Senator Lester Hunt
WordsWorth Publishing (2013)

The Sagebrush Gospel
WordsWorth Publishing (2014)

The Man in the Arena:
The Life and Times of U.S. Senator Gale McGee
University of Nebraska/Potomac Press (2018)

ISBN-13: 978-0-9896405-7-2

Cover photo of the fence near Laramie where Matthew Shepard was left to die, courtesy of the Matthew Shepard Foundation.

Cover and book design by Renée C. Tafoya

Published by WordsWorth. Cody, Wyoming

Printed in the U.S.A.

For Lois

CONTENTS

PROLOGUE

Twenty years ago, a nationally-known sports columnist wrote a book entitled "Tuesday's with Morie." Mitch Albom wrote about the days he spent visiting a former professor, a 78-year-old man named Morrie Schwartz who was dying of amyotrophic lateral sclerosis or ALS or "Lou Gehrig's Disease." Albom recounted the life's lessons he learned spending those "Tuesdays with Morrie.

From the spring of 2016 until Lois became incapacitated and subsequently died from a brain tumor in the early winter weeks of 2017, she and I spent nearly every Monday afternoon together. Those "Mondays with Lois" began when she invited me to write her memoir. Actually, Lois first asked me to do that in 2014. I had just completed *"Dying for Joe McCarthy's Sins: The Suicide of Wyoming Senator Lester Hunt."* Lois liked the book and had read several of the weekly columns I write for the *Wyoming Tribune-Eagle.* She knew I shared many of her concerns about cultural, political, religious and racial attitudes in Wyoming. Lois asked me to write her story. Initially, I declined, explaining to Lois that I never wanted to write books. I only wanted to tell Senator Hunt's story.

Early in 2016, Lois renewed her request. By then, Lois was clearer in her own mind about what she wanted in a book. She wanted to tell the story of her grandparents and how they came to Wyoming from Finland in the 1800s and how tough their lives were. She wanted to tell the story of her parents who made a life for their family in Rock Springs, and Winton, Wyoming. Lois wanted to tell her own story too. She wanted other women to know the lessons of how she fought her way through gender-based discrimination and accomplished extraordinary things.

Most of all, Lois wanted to tell the truth about "the Equality State." During her lifetime, Lois was painfully aware of the failure of her state to live up to that lofty motto. From the time she was a child, she had read Wyoming history books touting the state's accomplishments for women. As an adult, she figured out those books were often written by "cheerleaders" and were less than honest about the reality of life in the state for women and cultural, racial, and religious minorities. Lois asked me if I'd be willing to write her memoir in a way that provided a complete and honest analysis of this history in the context of her own life.

I heard her out, signed on, and began my "Mondays with Lois."

Just as Mitch Albom learned life lessons in his "Tuesdays with Morrie," I learned from Lois. Each time we met, it seemed her memories of life in Wyoming turned over old stones, some heavier than others. I had been superficially aware of the tough lives of late 1800s and early 1900s Wyoming coal miners. Now, I saw their stories through the eyes of a child who watched her farther go off to work each day in one of the world's most dangerous of occupations, wondering whether he would come home alive. I learned through Lois's story about poverty in Wyoming and how the vision parents have for their children can lift them out of that condition.

Lois was clear about how she didn't live life in a bubble. Events recounted in Wyoming history provided a context to her life. Her 4th grade teacher may have taught her that this is "the Equality State," but she saw it through a different, more honest lens.

On the day before Lois was moved from the hospital to hospice, a legislative committee met to discuss a simple bill proposing to change gender-based language such as "husband and wife" to gender-neutral terms such as "spouse" or "married couple." The proposal sought to amend statutes such as those governing retirement benefits for firefighters. Current law speaks only about benefits for "wives" as though there are no female fighters. Seemed simple enough.

It wasn't. It got ugly when a group of right-wing religious fanatics gathered in their churches to plan their testimony. It was like the KKK once gathered in Southern churches to plan a lynching. Public discussions of matters such as this provide observers with continual reminders that Wyoming is indeed the state where a gay man was murdered and others the subject of heinous treatment. One of the religionists saw non-existent boogeymen in the proposed legislation. Aware that he was seated across from State Representative Cathy Connolly, the only openly lesbian in the Wyoming legislature, but apparently unaware that the U.S. Supreme Court had long ago made same-sex marriage legal, he figured this bill was intended to accomplish that. He asked "What will next constitute a union? A man and his sister? You know, a man and his dog?"[1] It's people like this who try to make certain that gays, lesbians, transgender and bisexual citizens are kept in their places and never allowed to feel equal in the Equality State. It's people like this who want to make sure Wyoming is never really the Equality State.

This restatement of Wyoming attitudes came at a prescient moment. It was as if the heavens were telling us that Lois's story mattered more now than ever and needed to be told even though she wouldn't be here to see the book published.

I am deeply saddened that Lois didn't live to see her book. She and I both expected she would make the rounds in Wyoming, presenting her book and making a case for change. She could have done so with grace, courage and eloquence. But, fate had other plans for Lois. At the time she became incapacitated, we had completed and she had read and approved nearly all of this book with the exception of this Prologue and some editing to update the manuscript after her death. I visited her while she was in the Davis Hospice Center in Cheyenne. The lamp of her eyes had not yet gone out. I had a sense that she could hear me and approved when I assured her the story would be told.

In earlier weeks, as Lois finished reading the manuscript, she smiled devilishly and said to me, "You and I are going to catch a lot of hell for this." I hope she was right. Even as God rests her soul, I know she would hope that this book might stir the souls of the living, that the hopeful notes sounded by Wyoming's motto might one day ring true.

As for me, I have God to thank for all those delightful "Mondays with Lois."

MOTTONEN, LOIS, CHEYENNE,
PRIVATE INTERMENT AT LAKEVIEW CEMETERY

That and a detailed obituary was the notice given her friends and others that Lois had left us. Lois was clear. She wanted no public funeral. She wanted no gathering of grieving friends and was laid to rest with no deserved fanfare. There was no funeral service. Thus, this book is her eulogy.

FOREWORD
BY RODGER MCDANIEL

IT'LL SHAKE YOUR NERVES AND RATTLE YOUR BRAIN

At the end of the 20th century, a panel of esteemed Wyoming historians evaluated the great news stories of the preceding 100 years. The panel included Dr. Phil Roberts, Mike Massie, Dr. David Kathka, Bob Righter, Mark Junge, John Albanese, Don Hodgson, Patty Myers, Dr. Michael Cassity, Loren Jost, and Roy Jordan. By any measure these women and men are well qualified to make thoughtful judgments about the state's history.[2]

Looking back over the period of time from 1900 to 2000, they evaluated all of the thousands of stories that contributed to Wyoming's history, rendering a judgment about which were the top ten Wyoming narratives of the century.

Their conclusions call into question the basis for referring to Wyoming as "The Equality State." Some will be less surprised than others to learn that the "Equality State's treatment of women was deemed the most important." Furthermore, three of the top ten stories this panel identified dealt with the unjust treatment Wyoming dealt out to women and racial minorities including First Nations People or Native Americans.

Panelist Roy Jordan, a Northwest Community College historian said, "There's been no conviction or commitment to women's rights throughout our whole history." Ranked fourth on the list was Wyoming's "mistreatment of minorities." The panel cited a great deal of evidence including Heart Mountain Relocation Center, the Black 14 incident at the University of Wyoming, and the murder of Matthew Shepard. The seventh ranked story centered on the "mistreatment of Indians." Ironically, "the continuing strong identification with cowboys" finished eighth.

That explains the title of this book. It is a blurring of two books, one fiction, the other not. The time has come for Howard Zinn to meet Wyoming. The two will become acquainted through the life story of Lois Mottonen. Professor Zinn, now a deceased historian, playwright, and activist, wrote "A People's History of the United States: 1492-Present." He was one of the brave historians in recent history to take an honest look at U.S. history. He did so through the lenses of the "working people, women, people of color, and organized social movements shaping our history."[3]

When Lois asked me to write this book, she said that was precisely what she was looking for, a Zinn-type history of the state. Her life and those of her immigrant parents span the years from the end of the 19th century into the 21st. Lois Mottonen is, by all measures, an extraordinary woman. Raised by resolute 2nd generation Finnish immigrants, she was taught the importance of a good education and determined work ethic. Growing up in Rock Springs and Winton, Wyoming, Lois's childhood was bathed in the diversity those historic mining communities afforded. At an early age, she felt the sting of gender-based discrimination but persisted in obtaining the education she knew she would need.

Lois Mottonen has enjoyed a stellar career, albeit hard earned. After receiving an accounting degree with honors at the University of Wyoming, Lois ran into the glass ceiling of sexism but maneuvered her way through the barriers and lived out an accomplished career as the first woman appointed to a top-level position in the Internal Revenue Service. Lois was the second Wyoming woman to become a Certified Public Accountant and organized the Wyoming Chapter of the American Society of Women Accountants in order to advocate for the rights of women in her profession. Lois also served as President of the 5,000 member American Women's Society of Certified Public Accountants. She won a Ford Foundation Fellowship to the University of Virginia. In recognition of her accomplished career, Lois was named a University of Wyoming Distinguished Alumni.

This memoir chronicles Lois's other professional and personal accomplishments in the context of Wyoming's historic marginalization of women. This book is not about settling any scores for those times when Lois's career path was blocked by sexism. Her parents and early life experiences prepared her to overcome those obstacles. It is, however, a call for others to recognize that many equally qualified women as well as ethnic, cultural, and religious minorities have found the Equality State anything but.

Lois has witnessed the truth of what that panel of Wyoming historians found. Wyoming has too often provided an unkind environment for women, cultural, racial, and religious minorities. Howard Zinn's analysis of U.S. history offers a road map for looking at Wyoming's. Zinn suggested readers "tick off one, two, three, four, five lovely things about America that we don't want disturbed."

> *"But if we have learned anything in the past 10 years, it is that these lovely things about America were never lovely. We have been expansionist and aggressive and mean to other people from the beginning. And we've been aggressive and mean to people in this country, and we've allocated the wealth of this country in a very unjust way. We've never had justice in the courts for the poor people, for black people, for radicals. Now how can we boast that America is a very special place? It is not that special. It really isn't."*[4]

That can be said of Wyoming and the "lovely" legends, myths, and symbols about the state that have so often substituted for facts and a reflective, Zinn-like history. If you think Wyoming is "the Equality State," hang around places where laws are debated or city ordinances ratified. Listen to the dialogue. Hear the words come from the mouths of those who run the state and make its political decisions. In the words of Jerry Lee Lewis, it'll shake your nerves and it'll rattle your brain. Most of all, it will empty you of the rhetoric employed to maintain any illusions about equality in Wyoming. That's why this book imagines Howard Zinn and Lois

Mottonen fist fighting in the Equality State.

Sherman Alexie's classic, "The Lone Ranger and Tonto Fistfight in Heaven," provided readers a glimpse into the sort of cultural skirmishes Lois witnessed in her lifetime in Wyoming and the extent to which symbols and images built a non-existent reality. Many readers will recall the 1950s television and radio show "The Lone Ranger and Tonto." The two men from different cultures teamed up to challenge evil in the Wild West. They always won but it didn't come easy. It took a fight. So, this book, "Howard Zinn and Lois Mottonen Fistfight in the Equality State," is an attempt to put up a fight so that we can see the real history of how women and racial, ethnic, religious, and intellectual minorities are treated and the cultural wars that undermine the myths. This book poses for Wyoming the troubling question Alexie asked in his 2017 poem entitled "Hymn."[5]

> *But, how much do you love the strange and the stranger?*
> *Hey, Caveman, do you see only danger*
> *When you peer into the night? Are you afraid*
> *Of the country that exists outside your cave?*
> *Hey, Caveman, when are you going to evolve?*
> *Are you still afraid of the way the earth revolves*
> *Around the sun and not the other way around?*
> *Are you terrified of the ever-shifting ground?*

Through two generations, Lois and her parents witnessed Wyoming's entire history from statehood until Lois's death. This book is her "fistfight" to tell the truth as she and her parents lived it.

If you find historical or other errors in the book they are mine. However, the perspective belongs to Lois.

Sherman Alexie said the title of his book came to him in a dream. The title of this book came to me from reading Zinn and Alexie and spending countless engaging hours listening to Lois tell the story of her nine decades of living in Wyoming.

FOREWORD
BY LOIS MOTTONEN

Dear reader, what follows is a memoir. Mine. My friend Rodger McDaniel wrote the words but the thoughts and opinions are mine alone. I have long been interested in writing my memoir; not so much my autobiography. The latter always seemed to me to be little more than a chronologically-linear regurgitation of dates and places. Writing an autobiography offered little more than an opportunity than to recount my personal history. The facts that I was born and raised in Rock Springs, Wyoming to second generation Finnish immigrants and ended up living most of my life 250 miles east of there in Cheyenne says little to nothing about my real-life experiences. It doesn't seem to be anything that would hold my attention, much less that of those I hope will take a few hours out of their lives to read this.

A memoir is different. Writing one means giving myself and the readers a chance to look beyond a recitation of biographical information and into the wider world that shaped my own life and quite possibly yours as well. A memoir permits me to tell my story, the story of a life lived entirely in the context of much of the history of Wyoming.

Literary experts say the assertions contained in a memoir should be considered factual. My memoir is a bit like the Bible in that between the covers of this book, you'll find a combination of history and legend, a myth or two, tales of patriarchy and matriarchy, some poetry and a healthy dose of the Gospel according to Lois. And, not unlike the Bible, the writing may be attributed to me but has actually been accomplished with the help of someone else. Rodger McDaniel is as close as most people in the state to being a native. An ordained minister of 20 years, he earlier served in the state legislature for a decade and was nominated for the United States Senate before practicing law for 22 years. He has observed Wyoming from several perches, political, religious, and cultural. Rodger has written three books previously and critiques his state in a weekly column published in the *Wyoming Tribune-Eagle*.

This memoir is mine but is the result of hundreds of hours I have spent with Rodger sorting through my more than 80 years in our state.

Unlike the Bible, there is no claim that the Holy Spirit inspired any of what's ahead. It was inspired only by my sense that someone should weave together the story of their life with a deeper sense of what it means to live it in the so-called Equality State.

In the final analysis, this memoir speaks my truth. It was Pilate who asked Jesus, "What is truth?" To some extent it is subjective. My truth may not be yours, though I'm guessing the truth of my experience correlates with that of many other Wyoming people, particularly women of my socio-economic and professional background. Certainly, there will be those for whom Wyoming was an entirely different experience. Wyoming is not unlike John Godfrey Saxe's story of "The Blind Men and the Elephant."

> *It was six men of Indostan*
> *to learning much inclined,*
> *who went to see the elephant,*
> *though all of them were blind,*
> *that each by observation*
> *might satisfy his mind.*

Like those six blind men, each of us has touched and been touched by certain aspects of Wyoming's economic and political culture, unique to the individual, in ways that create an image of the state in each of our minds. Like fingerprints, no two are the same, though there are intersections. To those whose ancestors came here early and acquired land and wealth, Wyoming has been an entirely different experience from that of the men and women who worked for and were oftentimes exploited by those same people. Wyoming is equally different for those who have the power to define it as the Equality State as opposed to the thousands who have lived the illusion of equality.

In what follows, I have attempted to give context to my life. What fuels this memoir is my sense that nothing happens in any of our lives that doesn't have its genesis in events that may seem disconnected but are not. For example, my grandparents didn't emigrate from Finland to the United States in a vacuum. Their choices, or lack of choices, are inextricably bound to Russian history and decisions made by a Czar. Likewise, the story of my father's death from Black lung disease doesn't begin on the day his doctors diagnosed the presence of the dreaded disease. That story begins when the Union Pacific and other mining companies sent men like my father into the mines, knowing but denying and covering up the risks, denials that carried the weight necessary to skew the medical science in such a way that they could plausibly deny any responsibility. My own experience in coming up against Wyoming's glass ceiling is but one piece of a larger puzzle, which when pieced together exposes the illusion that Wyoming is the Equality State.

Accordingly, this memoir identifies the intersections of my experience with the history of Wyoming. As I tell my story, I suspect many of you will see your own.

1   Andrew Graham, "Unduly Cruel: Gender language debate turns ugly," December 5, 2017, http://www.wyofile.com/unduly-cruel-gender-language-debate-turns-ugly/?utm_source=newsletter&utm_medium=email&utm_campaign=weeklynewsletter, accesses December 5, 2017.

2   "*Wyoming History News*," Published by Members of the Wyoming State Historical Society, Vol. 47, Number 1 (February 2000).

3   Bill Moyers, Full Text: Howard Zinn's "The Problem Is Civil Disobedience" November 1970 http://billmoyers.com/story/howard-zinn-social-justice/#. WYK1vX5uUZQ.facebook, accessed July 31, 2017.

4   "The Problem is Civil Disobedience," Moyers.

5   "Hymn: A new Poem by Sherman Alexie," https://earlybirdbooks.com/hymn-a-new-poem-by-sherman-alexie, Accessed December 28, 2017.

CHAPTER ONE

A DELUSION WITHIN AN ILLUSION

An illusion is not an easy thing to grasp. Illusions are not created overnight. Illusions differ from myth. Myths contain fundamental truths. Illusions deny them. People with the power to create illusions have a great deal at stake in making them appear to be reality. A great deal of time and money, as well as personal reputations, are expended in creating and maintaining illusions. When successful, those who create illusions come to believe they are real. Indeed, that is what makes them so intransigent and punishing to dispel. Thus, it was as though calling it the "Equality State" made it so.

Soren Kierkegaard, the 17th century Danish poet and theologian described how this occurs. In as much as Mr. Kierkegaard died nearly four decades before Wyoming became a state, he could not have been talking about the "Equality State." And yet he was.

Kierkegaard believed that challenging illusions was risky if not dangerous. He came to realize that illusions should not be challenged directly, but only indirectly, if at all. "One must approach from behind the person who is under the illusion."[6] Sam Western chose to approach deluded persons directly. He said they had been "Pushed off the mountain and sold down the river."[7] Western's book by that title courageously noted that Wyoming "just can't face its past," choosing instead to "bury" its history.[8] Western blamed much of it on what he called Wyoming's "burly mythology of independence." It's hard to argue with Sam Western's well-thought-out premise, but Wyoming also entertains a burly mythology of equality. The state is unable to handle the truth and it is found in the tension between wanting to be known as "The Equality State" and not actually being willing to become "The Equality State." It's one of those illusions that Soren Kierkegaard thought difficult to dispel.

Wyoming was not yet even a state when illusion-making began.

The illusion started early. Indeed, it could be better described as a delusion within an illusion. Wyoming was a new U.S. territory when the all-male membership of the territorial legislature thought it might help convince the Congress to award statehood to Wyoming if women were given the right to vote. And so, the First Territorial Legislature enacted a bill providing, "Every woman of the age of twenty-one years residing in this territory, may, at every election cast her vote; and her right to the elective franchise and to hold office under the election laws of the territory shall be the same as those of electors."[9]

The population of the Wyoming territory then included only 9000 folks of European ancestry and the "hostile Indians (who) still roamed the Plains." One of the state's early 20th century historians said, "The adventurers and desperadoes that floated in with the incoming settlers had nothing to do with making the laws. They were transients and pilgrims. The real bona fide first settlers of Wyoming were men of sterling character, broad vision, and undoubted courage." I.S. Bartlett said these "adventurers and desperadoes" learned the "lessons of liberty and equality" in a rather odd way; fighting the Civil War under Lee, Jackson, Sherman, and Grant. Bartlett determined that experience gave Wyoming a group of men who held women in "lofty respect," who also enacted laws giving women property rights and guaranteeing female school teachers would earn as much as men.[10]

Across the country, there was growing support for the idea of allowing women, at least white women, to vote. Bills had been introduced in Congress and a number of state legislatures. A few narrowly failed to be enacted. Wyoming historian T.A. Larson explained, "Conditions were ripe for a legislative victory somewhere. The Wyoming legislators had the options of jumping in at the head of the parade or of watching it go by." They tried to have it both ways.

Wyoming historian Tom Rea found some legislators had a less than egalitarian motive, arising not from the "lessons of liberty and equality" learned while fighting the Civil War. Rea wrote, "Many of the legislators believed strongly that if blacks and Chinese were to have the vote, then women, especially white women, should have it, too." Rea's research located a Cheyenne newspaper article that "reported this as 'the clincher' argument. 'Damn it," an unnamed legislator supposedly said, 'if you are going to let the niggers (sic) and the pigtails (sic) vote, we will ring in the women, too."[11]

Legend has it that one of the foremost advocates for women's rights invited 20 of the men she thought most influential in Wyoming's new Territorial government to a dinner party at her home. There, Esther Hobart Morris made an impassioned appeal for their state to "jump in at the head of the parade." William H. Bright was invited. Ben Sheeks was not. The slight would have unintended consequences.

The bill was sponsored by lawmaker Bright of South Pass. Bright was one of those Civil War veterans who landed in Wyoming after the war. At the time the bill was introduced, it allowed women age 18 and older to vote. A South Pass colleague, Ben Sheeks, a snarly opponent of women's suffrage made an attempt to amend the bill to allow "all colored women and squaws (sic)" to vote. When that failed, he succeeded in amending the bill to raise the voting age to 21 years. The bill then passed. Wyoming's white women were given the right to vote. The *Cheyenne Leader* newspaper dubbed Col. Bright "immortal."

However immortal Bright may have been and however "lofty" his fellow legislators respect for women might have been at the moment, the ink was barely dry on the act giving them the right to vote when most of the territorial legislators suffered a change of heart about suffrage. Democratic party control during the First Territorial Legislature shifted to Republican control for the Second, putting a woman's right to vote on the chopping block.

The minority party leader who led the opposition in the First Territorial Legislature was now the powerful Speaker of the House. He was Ben Sheeks, the same man left off of Esther Hobart Morris's dinner invitation list. Sheeks argued with vitriol that the original measure had been passed "thoughtlessly, and without proper consideration." His bill to undo a woman's right to vote quickly passed both houses of the legislature. However, it was vetoed by the Governor. Governor A.J. Campbell said in his veto message, "Surely the ability to judge and determine, the power of choice, does not depend upon sex." A two-thirds majority of the House disagreed. They voted to override the veto. But Wyoming's "Equality State" motto was salvaged by a one-vote margin when the Council (then the name of the state senate) upheld the veto 5-4, one vote short of the 2/3rds required to override.[12]

However, it's been a tough ride ever since for those who believe the Equality State should be the equality state. Yes, it's true that within a few months after the legislature gave women the right to vote, one of them, Esther Hobart Morris, became the first woman ever appointed to be a justice of the peace. In 1924, Nellie Tayloe Ross was the first female to ever be elected Governor. Ask a Wyomingite why the state is called the Equality State and you'll hear about things like that, events that happened decades ago.

That is the sort of illusion Kierkegaard said was so hard to overcome. While Wyoming may have earned the "Equality State" motto in the early days, a lot of ugly water has since flowed under that bridge. Unfortunately, Wyoming has a right-wing culture that is frequently detrimental to making it a good place to live for everyone. Remember the Black 14-incident at the University, the beating and hanging on a fence of a young gay man in Laramie a few years ago, and most recently powerful oil and mining interests that contributed sufficient amounts of money to the University of Wyoming that they could force the removal and destruction of a piece of art, which they found offensive, from the campus?

There is little or no evidence to back up the state motto more recent than Nellie Tayloe Ross's 1925 election as the nation's first woman Governor. Wyoming women have had little political power and Wyoming has neither offered nor honored diversity. As a result, the white Christian men who broker the state's power never felt particularly compelled to protect the political or economic rights of ethnic, gender, religious, or sexual minorities. All the while the state feigned a certain amount of pride in its motto. Spoiler alert: Wyoming really isn't the "Equality" state. As a woman, I know.

The motto has served as a shield against thoughtful proposals to rein in discrimination. For many, the motto has served as a substitute for genuine equality, an irony encountered frequently in daily Wyoming life. The greatest irony is how the statue of Esther Hobart Morris stands at the entrance of the State Capitol building in a place that lawmakers pass by as they ascend the steps on their way to the House and Senate chambers where they make certain equality remains nothing more than an illusion.

This memoir attempts to do what Kierkegaard suggested. It does not challenge "directly but only indirectly" the illusion that Wyoming is the Equality State. It does so by telling the story of the life of one woman. The Mottonens (pronounced "Mah-toh-nens") came here from Finland in the last years of the 19th century. I was born in Wyoming in the early years of the Great Depression and became a product of Wyoming's education system. Later, as the so-called women's movement was gaining momentum, I became a professional woman and learned what it meant to be a woman in the Equality State for a majority of the years Wyoming has been a state. I lived and survived the illusion of equality. Along the way I learned no one's life is their own. None of us lives in isolation from the lives of others, even those we never meet.

---

6   Soren Kierkegaard, *The Point of View for My Work as an Author"* Unpublished during the writer's lifetime, Harper Torchbooks-The Cloister Library (1962), 24-25.

7   Sam Western, *Pushed Off the Mountain, Sold Down the River,* Denver, San Francisco and Moose, Wyoming, Homestead Publishing (2002).

8   *Pushed Off the Mountain,* 12.

9   *History of Wyoming,* Vol. 1, Edited by I.S. Bartlett, Chicago-S.J. Clark Publishing Co. (1918), 197.

10   Bartlett, *History of Wyoming,* 197-198.

11   Tom Rea, "Right Choice, Wrong Reasons: Wyoming Women Win the Right to Vote" http://www.wyohistory.org/essays/right-choice-wrong-reasons-wyoming-women-win-right-vote#sthash.0Dxa0Axd.dpuf.

12   *"Wyoming-From Territorial Days to the Present"* Vol. 1, Edited by Francis Birkhead Beard, The American Historical Society, Inc. Chicago and New York (1933), 241-242.

CHAPTER TWO

INSTRUCTIONS FOR BREWING BEER, IMPREGNATION BY CONSUMPTION OF A LINGONBERRY AND, OF COURSE, SEVERAL SUICIDES

This memoir could not be written but for "a lass, an air-girl, a nice nature daughter," a Russian Czar, and the rotting corpses of prehistoric plants.

My beginnings are, as are yours, mythological. We Finns tell the story of the time long ago when there was a lass who was pregnant for "seven hundred years, nine ages of man." As only a woman who has given birth might imagine, the predicament caused her great pain and consternation. She rolled in the waters, swimming east, west, northwest and south but could not shake the "fiery birth-pangs." Still no creature was born. Like the white dove dispatched by the God of the Hebrews to help Noah find dry land after the Great Flood, another bird arrived in the midst of my ancestors' "creation" story. It searched for a nesting place, flying east, west, northwest and south. Still, it found no place to either rest or nest.

Then the water mother, the air-lass one and the same, raised her knees out of the sea. The bird saw it was a place to light. On her kneecap, it finally landed. There it built a nest and laid six eggs of gold and one of iron. Soon they began to hatch. First one opened and then another. Soon a third. The water-mother's skin felt ablaze and she jerked her knees and shook her limbs. The movement caused the remaining eggs to roll into the water where they smashed into bits and broke into pieces.

The bits and pieces "changed into good things." The lower half of one egg became Mother Earth while its upper half became heaven above. The yolk became "the sun for shining" while the upper part that was white "became the moon for gleaming." Finally, so the myth teaches, that which "in an egg is mottled became the stars in the sky, what in an egg was blackish became the clouds of the air."

Additional ages passed before the water mother lifted her head from the sea to form sea creatures. Her foot dragged the bottom of the sea to dig out fish troughs. When she turned on one side, she formed the smooth shores and the salmon haunts and shaped the bays, the crags in the water and the hidden reefs that would become haunted sites of shipwrecks.

The myth's hero had yet to make an appearance. "But still Väinämöinen remained unborn. He "went round his mother's womb for thirty summers and as many winters." Väinämöinen finally emerged as the central character, hero, and wise old man with the magical voice in Finnish folklore and the epic poem "Kalevala" (pronounced "Kall-eh-vala). He becomes "the old Väinämöinen" as the story consumes nearly 700 pages and 50 poems.[13] The poems' finality heralds the end of pagan beliefs and the advent of Christianity in Finland.

Finnish humorist Tarja Moles describes the Kalevala.

> *"It's a 19th century poetry collection based on Karelian and Finnish mythology and oral tradition, with all the ingredients of a great story: shamanistic journey, unrequited love, magical singing that is more powerful in battle than (is) violence, slaver, the creation of a machine that brings fortunes to its owners, instructions for brewing beer, impregnation by consumption of a lingonberry and, of course, several suicides."[14]*

THE PERIOD OF RUSSIFICATION FOR THE SHEER SAKE OF RUSSIFICATION

The Kalevala provides the mythological context for the lives lived by my ancestors in Finland. For the explanation of how they got from Finland to Wyoming, one would have to study 19th century Russian history. Historians divide the history of Finland into three parts. First, until 1809, Finland was a part of the Swedish sphere. For slightly more than another century through 1917, Finland was under Russian control in varying degrees. Finland has since been independent.

My grandparents were born and lived in Finland during the second era. They were farmers. The family name can be traced far back into the first division of Finnish history to the mid 6th century and a fellow named Pietari Mottonen. He lived in Perho at the heart of Finland. A village named Mottonen lies not far from Perho. Archaeologists have located stone-age evidence of fishermen, hunters, and gatherers there. Archaeologists believe it was not until the time of Pietari's birth in the mid 1500s that permanent dwellings were erected in this part of Finland.[15]

One of Finland's great problems was an accident resulting from the way in which geography too often breeds politics. Finland, like so many other nations that end up as targets, was simply too close to the Russian border. Big nations like to have buffers from external threats. The United States has two oceans. Russia had Finland. So, it was that a couple of centuries after Pietari that the Russians invaded. What Finn historians call the Greater Wrath and the Lesser Wrath covered the Russian occupation of much of the 18th century.[16] In the first years of the 19th century, the Russian Emperor Alexander I fully conquered the Finns. Russians would more or less exercise control over the land until the Bolshevik Revolution of 1917.

It's that second period, "the period of Russification for the sheer sake of Russification,"[17] that led to the emigration of my ancestors from Finland and eventually to Wyoming. For most of the 19th century, although Russia controlled Finland, it allowed a useful measure of self-government. However, that changed in the turbulent years leading to 1901 when Czar Nicholas II issued an order dissolving the Finnish army and ordering its conscription as a part of the Russian military.

The result was a great deal of discord among Finns. Some Finns resisted while others acquiesced and adopted an attitude of compliance. Some, like Andrew and Hilma Matson and Karolina and Matti Mottonen, my grandparents, boarded ships headed for America. When Matti "renounced forever all allegiance and fidelity" to the Russian Czar, he was awarded U.S. citizenship by order of the State District Court Judge David Craig in Sweetwater

1904 photo of Karolina and Matti Mottonen and children (left to right) Julius, Nestori (Lois's father), and Wilho.

County, Wyoming on October 25, 1904. Andrew became a U.S. citizen years earlier when he swore that same oath of renunciation of the Czar and allegiance to America on October 3, 1896.

A HINTERLAND, POWERED BY WIND THAT ONCE DROVE PIONEER WOMEN INSANE

That's the point in time when the rotting corpses of 300 to 400 million-year-old plants became a part of this memoir. Because of their contribution, coal was here before the cowboys. Two hundred and forty million years before Matti and Andrew left the farm in Finland, at least 40 kinds of dinosaurs walked the part of the earth we know as Sweetwater County, Wyoming. It was the Mesozoic geologic period. Some were small, others quite large. Some could fly. Some swam. For the dinosaurs, the abundant vegetation was the Garden of Eden, hosting everything they needed among palm trees and magnolia.[18]

It all ended with a big bang, 65 million years before Matti and Andrew emigrated. A cataclysmic event, still not fully understood, destroyed the dinosaurs and most other then-existing plant life forms. "A widely accepted explanation associates the extinction with a large asteroid landing on what is now the north shore of the Yucatan Peninsula."[19] Dust clouds rose from the asteroid's landing site, covering the earth and blocking the warmth of the sun that was necessary for the continued life of the dinosaurs and the vegetation.

Characteristic of the early stages of the subsequent Cenozoic Age were large coastal swamps that reached into present day Wyoming. The surrounding environment was quite at war with itself. The temperatures regularly reached 100 degrees Fahrenheit or more, enabling the decay of the plants. Coal was formed in these swamps as the seas and waters slowly disappeared leaving the organic material from dead ferns, trees, and other ancient plants under the steaming silt. Unlike the swamps in what became the Eastern United States, the swamps in Wyoming contained little sulfur, creating the state's vaunted low-sulfur coal deposits.

And so, the book of the generations was written. In the beginning were the dinosaurs and the plants they ate. The Big Bang begat dust clouds that caused that plant and animal life to die off. Decomposing plants begat the coal. The coal begat the Union Pacific Railroad which begat the coal mines of Southeast Wyoming which begat the emigration of Andrew Matson and his wife Hilma Kingas and of Matti Mottonen and his wife Karolina Hirvikoski, which begat the marriage of Matti and Karolina's son Nestor and Andrew and Hilma's daughter Cecelia, which begat me.

It's not clear whether "at the beginning of God's creating of the heavens and the earth"[20] God gave that much thought to the 100,000 square miles near the center of North America that would one day be known as Wyoming. I have traveled it all. It is true that parts of Wyoming are among the most beautiful of all the earth's 197 million square miles. Other parts, not so much. The state's 30 million acres range from the most alluring landscapes to the most desolate moonscapes. Think about it this way. With just a little divine tweaking, the elevation of Wyoming's high plains could have been lowered just enough to have made millions of those acres less arid, frigid, and windy and more productive for farmers, ranchers, and others. The Creator could have made it a little less like the Wyoming poet Michelle Irwin described when she wrote, "At first glance, a hinterland, more antelope than men, powered by wind that once drove pioneer women insane."[21]

Furthermore, the Creator's decision to deposit vast amounts of oil, coal, natural gas, trona, and uranium under Wyoming's arid, sometimes frigid, always harsh and windy surface preordained that the state would be little more than an economic colony for the world's largest corporations and their wealthy, elite owners. The state has made a lot of people quite wealthy even though many of them never set foot on its land.

However, it wasn't God's decisions that did all of that. Unless you read the first two chapters of Genesis as science, you realize that what God did on Day One was not to think through every detail about how the land and waters would one day appear. God was far more interested in bringing some order to the chaos than about the ability of Wyoming people to make a living 13 billion years later. God was more focused on setting in motion a billions-of-years long geologic process. Once released, that process assumed control. From the time "the world was wild and waste, darkness over the earth, rushing Spirit of God hovering over the face of the waters"[22] until the mountains and plains of Wyoming first appeared as they do today, perhaps nine billion years came and went. Billions more would come and go before farming, ranching, and mining mattered.

In fact, if the entirety of the history of the Universe were scaled to the size of a football field, depicting the beginning to be on our goal line, Wyoming's place would be nearly one hundred yards away, at an indecipherably small distance from our opponent's goal line. As difficult as it may be for those who run the state today, Wyoming mattered not even a little for nearly all of the world's history. And yet, all of those more than 13.8 billion years that came before statehood made us what we are today.

DESTINED TO BECOME ONE OF THE
RICHEST STATES IN THE UNION

The first of the Mottonens arrived in the United States in 1888. Andrew came first. Next were the women. Hilma and Karolina came from Finland in 1892. Matti Mottonen arrived in 1897. They found the original Wyoming Territory cobbled together from pieces of the Louisiana Purchase, the northern edges of the Mexico and Texas cession, and parts of the Washington, Dakota and Oregon Territories. Two years after Andrew Matson arrived from Finland, Wyoming became the 44th state in the Union. Wyoming's oft-harsh early winter weather nearly derailed statehood. Yogi Berra famously said that no matter who you are, it will be the weather that determines the size of your funeral. The same can be said for voter turnout in a Wyoming election.

A snowstorm engulfed the state on the day voters went to the polls to answer the question of whether or not to adopt a proposed state constitution. The previous year more than 18,000 turned out to vote for delegates to the convention who were charged with writing the constitution. But on November 4, 1889, fewer than half of that number ventured to the polls in a statehood plebiscite. On that day, 6,272 voted in favor while 1,923 opposed the new constitution. Congress later debated whether it was the weather and not indifference that resulted in such minimal voter participation.[23] Wyoming's Congressional Delegate Joseph Carey had been fudging the numbers, telling colleagues his state had as many as 120,000 residents. His exaggeration made it even more difficult to explain why fewer than seven percent of that number cast ballots.

Even so, there were supporters in the Nation's capital. Members of the 1890 Congress supporting statehood for Wyoming advised the United States Senate that, in their view, Wyoming would most certainly become "a strong, prosperous, and progressive state."[24] In the intervening years, it has at times, been strong and prosperous between economic busts.

Congress duly noted Wyoming's mineral, petroleum, and coal riches. "The mineral wealth of the Territory can scarcely be comprehended and from this source alone it is destined to become one of the richest states in the Union." The report recommending statehood went on to proclaim that, "Few states, if any, have been admitted to the Union which at the date of admission had as much actual wealth as Wyoming."

The glowing report read like Garrison Keillor's Lake Wobegon where "all the women are strong, the men are good looking and the all the children are above average." The citizens of the proposed state were said to be enterprising, its Indians not "warlike," its winters neither "severe nor long," its people above average in education and "general habits," and its scenic features "remarkable." The report stretched its claim about Women's Suffrage saying it "is favored by both political parties."[25] Nonetheless, there were detractors such as Missouri Senator George Graham Vest who is best remembered for his 1869 "tribute to a dog." Senator Vest orated,

> *"A man's reputation may be sacrificed in a moment of ill-considered action. The people who are prone to fall on their knees to do us honor when success is with us may be the first to throw the stone of malice when failure settles its cloud upon our heads. The one absolutely unselfish friend that a man can have in this selfish world, the one that never deserts him and the one that never proves ungrateful or treacherous is his dog."*

Senator Vest may have had a soft spot for dogs but not for Wyoming statehood. He said there was a time when the admission of a Territory was "a matter of considerable public importance." The Missourian lamented that those days were gone and that now statehood was granted, "in bunches."[26] He worried there were not enough people in the Wyoming Territory and that most of them were men, as they "must be from the nature of the country and the necessities of their surroundings." Although the Democrat was concerned that Wyoming's two Senators would likely be Republicans he complained about a particular provision in Wyoming's new constitution.

> *No distinction shall ever be made by law between resident aliens and citizens as to the possession, taxation, enjoyment and descent of property.*[27]

Senator Vest was beside himself. "Every Senator who votes for the admission of this state with that provision in its bill of rights says to the people of Europe, to the alien capitalists, to their nomadic noblemen who come here and buy vast possessions on which to settle their younger sons, 'Wyoming is open to you, and if your money holds out you can buy two-thirds of the entire state.'"[28]

There were other objections. The wildly-bearded Senator James Kimbrough Jones of Arkansas didn't agree with Wyoming's compulsory education provision. "It may be very good," he told his colleagues, "to compel a man to join my church and to make him think as I do about religion...but this idea of compulsory education is not American."[29]

The greater debate focused on that election when so few voters braved the snow to turn out to approve the proposed constitution. Wyoming had yet to establish its current tradition of low voter participation. Today, nearly four out of ten eligible Wyoming voters never even trouble themselves to register. But, back then low voter turnout was scandalous. Some saw something darker than snow. The allegations included charges of voter fraud. Senator Jones offered an article from a Wyoming newspaper. It was said that on the day of the election, no public vote was held in Newcastle. Instead "three persons, each of whom we could name, went into a backroom and conducted a cigar-box election." The men allegedly cast all the ballots in favor of the constitution but then decided there should be a few contrary votes. Thus, Newcastle reported a tally of 493-7. Senator Jones thought that alone should nullify the statehood bill.

At long last, Senators got around to taking about the elephant in the room. It was John Henninger Reagan of Texas. "Mr. President," his voice boomed in sermonic grandeur, "when the Almighty created men and women he made them for different purposes, and 6,000 years (the Biblical dating of the beginning of the universe) of experience have recognized the wisdom and justice of the Almighty in this arrangement." Senator Reagan believed the Territorial legislature in Wyoming had substituted its knowledge for that of the Creator. It displeased him greatly. "How is it possible," he asked, "that women can be clothed with the duties and responsibilities of men and at the same time perform the natural and necessary duties of women." He figured there would not be "much happiness in the home" if women were "making speeches, electioneering with voters, and pushing their way to the polls."[30]

Other Senators were quick to point out that even the Constitution of the United States described members of Congress with a masculine pronoun. What more did they need to know? That seemed determinative to some. The Constitution said what it meant and meant what it said. These were the ancestors of 21st century jurists like the late U.S. Supreme Court Justice Antonin Scalia, a legal originalist, who said, "The Constitution that I interpret is not living but dead." For them, the Constitution died on the day its framers employed masculine pronouns when talking of Members of Congress. "Shes" were not included. It should not be now resurrected, they thought, in order to engage in social experimentation.

Alabama Senator John Tyler Morgan opened a lengthy debate when he inquired, "Now, when your female Representative comes into the House from the State of Wyoming, how will you get along with" a provision of the U.S. Constitution that uses the pronoun "he" when referring to U.S. Representatives Senator Morgan continued, "I should dislike very much to see our magnificent looking Vice-President supplanted by the handsomest woman that might come even from Wyoming."

Mr. Morgan's fears were a long time being realized. It was 1916, a generation later, when that glass ceiling was shattered. Montana elected Jeanette Pickering Rankin, the first woman in Congress. In the entire history of the U.S. Senate, more than 2,000 people have been elected to that institution, which has been a decidedly male bastion. Only about 50 of them have been women.[31] Several of those were politely appointed to fill a seat held by a recently-deceased husband. The first woman elected to the Senate was Hattie Caraway, a prohibitionist who was the first woman to sponsor the Equal Rights Amendment to the U.S. Constitution.[32] It was 1922. Senator Caraway served until 1945 when she was succeeded by J. William Fulbright, one of the Senate's giants.

But Wyoming voters worshiped that masculine pronoun much longer. The state never sent a woman to the United States Senate. Mary Jane Bartlett, known by her husband's name Mrs. I.S. Bartlett, was nominated, though not selected by a legislative caucus to be a Senator in the days when state legislators, not the people chose them. It was 105 years after Senator Morgan worried about the day a "female Representative comes into the House from the

State of Wyoming" when Barbara Cubin was elected to Congress. Curiously, Wyoming hasn't since quit electing women to the House of Representatives.[33]

Finally, after the lengthy debate over whether foreigners should be able to buy Wyoming land, or whether children should be required to go to school, and whether women deserved to vote, the bill admitting Wyoming to the Union came to a final vote. More Senators were absent than voted for the bill, which passed 29-18. President William Henry Harrison, whose great-great grandson and namesake later served as a Wyoming Congressman, signed the bill into law on July 10, 1890.

THE MOST NOTORIOUS EVENT IN THE HISTORY OF WYOMING

My family emigrated to Wyoming during these significant times of the state's history. Andrew arrived just two years before Wyoming became the 44th state. Grandmother Hilma came to the state two years later at the time of the outbreak of what Dr. Taft Alfred Larson, the state's preeminent historian, called "the most notorious event in the history of Wyoming."[34]

The Johnson County War is the name given to a series of "murderous episodes" beginning in late 1891 and culminating in the full-scale invasion of the county in April 1892 by twenty-five cattlemen and their top hands along with another twenty-five hired guns."[35] The war took place in a part of the state about as far as one could get away from Diamondville where Andrew and Hilma were busy making their home. It was the sequel of sorts to the Biblical story of Cain and Abel in the fourth chapter of the Book of Genesis.

> *Eve bore his brother Abel. Now Abel was a keeper of sheep, and Cain a tiller of the ground. In the course of time Cain brought to the LORD an offering of the fruit of the ground, and Abel brought of the firstlings of his flock and of their fat portions. And the LORD had regard for Abel and his offering, but for Cain and his*

offering he had no regard. So, Cain was very angry,
and his countenance fell. — GENESIS 4

In this case the tensions arose between cattlemen and sheepmen, each of whom thought their lifestyle to have been blessed more than the other. It was the early Wyoming politicians that had regard for one, and not for the other, that led to brothers killing brothers. Jack R. Gage, a one-time Wyoming Governor and Secretary of State, was better known as a humorist. Mr. Gage wrote *The Johnson County War Is a Pack of Lies,* a delightful two-sided book about the Johnson County War. The reader opens one side titled "The Baron's Side" and reads their account of the incident. Turn the book over and upside down and you can read "The Rustler's Side."

The so-called "rustlers" were the little guys who, Gage wrote, felt they were "going to need a little help if they were going to stick it out in that country." As with much of history, the plot is far more complicated. In a nutshell, the "Barons" wanted to control as much land as possible and the "Rustlers" were trying to carve out a bit of it for themselves. When the Barons organized the invasion, the pretext was that the they had been victims of rustling campaigns, losing massive numbers of cattle. When they asked help from the criminal justice system, juries were partial to the "little guys" and so the Barons concluded, as barons have historically concluded, that they had to take the law into their own hands.

"The first step was the formation of an assassination squad comprised of employees of the Wyoming Stock Growers Association."[36] It was the beginning of the out-sized influence of the organization on all things Wyoming. Eventually these invaders ended up on the wrong side of the gun and were taken into custody where friendly politicians made sure the charges were dismissed. The Cheyenne lawyer who defended them was Willis Van Devanter, a close personal friend of the invaders' political protector Senator Francis E. Warren.

Legend has it that his role in convincing friendly judges to censor a book unfriendly to the Stockgrowers' version of the

War written by Asa Mercer was the chief stepping stone in Van Devanter's otherwise improbable path to the high court. That legend was recounted to the writer of this book by Congressman Teno Roncalio. The editors of a Wikipedia essay on the matter back up Roncalio's story of *The Banditti of the Plains* this way.

> *"The first edition of the book is one of the rarities of Western Americana. Immediately after it was printed the Wyoming cattlemen objected and sued. The court ordered it destroyed. While the books were in the court's custody, a large number were stolen and smuggled to Denver and later bound. For many years, the Wyoming Stockgrowers' Association, their sympathizers, and their descendants destroyed every copy they came across.*[37]

The Wikipedia essay tells of how Mercer was harassed and physically assaulted, his printing press demolished, his writing seized as "obscenity," and his business destroyed. The article is admittedly in need of citations to its assertions but conforms to the legend recited often by Wyoming Congressman Teno Roncalio, a man known for truthfulness and knowledge of Wyoming history.

As his reward for this and other favors he had granted Warren, Mr. Van Devanter was appointed to the United States Supreme Court in 1911. According to one Supreme Court historian, Van Devanter was afflicted with "pen paralysis" rarely writing anything for the Court in constitutional cases until his retirement in 1937.[38] Nonetheless, he was a thorn in President Franklin Roosevelt's side. As the President's New Deal was challenged in the courts, the Wyoming jurist was "a hindrance to the enactment of the more liberal approaches to alleviate the economic depression." Van Devanter was one of the chief reasons for FDR's controversial court packing scheme.

Regardless of how or whether he earned it, Justice Van Devanter is still the sole Wyomingite to have had the great honor of serving on the nation's highest court.

The war between the cattlemen and the sheep men didn't end with the Johnson County War. The cauldron boiled for years. About a decade later, on July 18, 1901, Tom Horn shot and killed 14-year-old Willie Nickell near Iron Mountain just outside of Cheyenne. Willie died for the sins of his father Kels. Those sins? Grazing sheep. Horn was convicted in what was then "the trial of the century." Tom Horn died for his own sins, hanging from the end of a rope in Cheyenne on November 20, 1903.

---

13   Elias Lonnrot, *The Kalevala: An Epic Poem After Oral Tradition*, Translated by Keith Bosley, Oxford University Press (1989).

14   Tarja Moles, *A Xenophobe's Guide to the Finns*, Published by Xenophobe's Guides (2011), 73.

15   History of Salamajärvi National Park, Prehistoric Hunters, http://www. nationalparks.fi/en/salamajarvinp/history, Accessed August 19, 2016.

16   http://www.sheppardsoftware.com/Europeweb/snapshot/Finland.htm, Accessed August 19, 2016.

17   Eino Jutikkala and Kauko Pirinen, *A History of Finland* (New York: Dorsett Press 1988), 195.

18   Dennis H. Knight, George P. Jones, William A. Reiners, and William H. Romme, *Mountains and Plains- The Ecology of Wyoming Landscapes 2nd Edition* (New Haven and London: Yale University Press 2014), 12-13.

19   Knight, *Mountains and Plains,* 13.

20   Genesis 1:1, *The Five Books of Moses-A New Translation with Introductions and Notes by Everett Fox,* Schocken Books (1997), 11.

21   Michelle Irwin, "Wyoming," "Blood, Water, Wind, and Stone: An Anthology of Wyoming Writers," Edited by Lori Howe, Sastrugi Press-San Diego and Jackson (2016), 8

22   Fox, *The Five Books of Moses,* Genesis 1:2, 13

23   *Congressional Record,* June 25, 1890, 6472

24   *Congressional Record,* June 25, 1890, 6472

25   *Congressional Record,* June 25, 1890, 6473

26   *Congressional Record,* June 25, 1890, 6483

27   *Wyoming Constitution,* Article 1, Section 29, which remains a part of the Constitution to this day.

28   *Congressional Record,* June 25, 1890, 6485

29   *Congressional Record,* June 25, 1890, 6517

30   *Congressional Record,* June 25, 1890, 6527

31   "Women in the U.S. Senate 1922-2015" (PDF). Center for American Women and Politics. Archived from the original (PDF) on 2015-07-03.

32   Nancy Hendricks, *Senator Hattie Caraway: An Arkansas Legacy*, The History Press (2013)

33   Barbara Cubin was sworn in to the U.S. House in 1995. She was followed by Cynthia Lummis in 2009 and Liz Cheney in 2017.

34   T.A. Larson, *History of Wyoming*, University of Nebraska Press (1995), 283.

35   John W. Davis, *Wyoming Range War-The Infamous Invasion of Johnson County*, Norman: University of Oklahoma Press (2010), ix.

36   "The Johnson County War: 1892 Invasion of Northern Wyoming" by John W. Davis, http://www.wyohistory.org/essays/johnson-county-war, A Project of the Wyoming State Historical Society; much of the information following this cite comes from this source.

37   https://en.wikipedia.org/wiki/Banditti_of_the_Plains

38   "Willis van Devanter [1859-1941]: Early Founder/Historic Leader" The New Netherland Institute, http://www.newnetherlandinstitute.org/history-and-heritage/dutch_americans/willis-van-devanter/ accessed November 14, 2016; and "Willis Van Devanter." *Oyez*. Chicago-Kent College of Law at Illinois Tech, n.d. Nov 13, 2016. <https://www.oyez.org/justices/willis_van_devanter>

CHAPTER THREE

ONE PESÄPAIKKA WAS KENILWORTH.
ANOTHER WAS DIAMONDVILLE, WYOMING

Within a few years of the end of the Johnson County War, after the invaders were comfortably out of jail and back home, the last of my grandparents arrived in America. The Mottonen migration was complete. Matti Mottonen came in 1897, after Andrew, Hilma, and Karolina. These four Finns were part of a significant emigration to the United States from late-19th century Finland, which extended roughly a half-a-century into the 1920s. Nearly 400,000 Finns crossed the Atlantic.[39] Once there, they became part of a Wyoming era witnessing the "largest single population gain in the history of the state."[40]

Before Matti and Andrew became coal miners, they were peasants, farming back home in Finland. Looking back farther, my ancestors came from the Central Ostrobothina region where farming was the chief occupation. Indeed, like the Matsons and the Mottonens, more than half of those leaving their Finnish homeland were farmers. Many Finns landed in states like Minnesota where they could earn a living with their farming skills. Others found jobs digging tunnels in the ground rather than tilling it. "Wyoming's first Finns arrived on the Union Pacific Railroad and began working in the coal-mining communities of Rock Springs."[41]

The more than 400,000 Finns coming to the U.S. ended up in communities as diverse as New York City, Minnesota and San Francisco among other places. Notoriously hard workers, they used their old-world skills to earn a living and provide for their families. Not many landed in Wyoming but then, that's true of all American settlers and other immigrants as well. Not many of anybody came and stayed in Wyoming's harsh environment, which is one reason the state remains today the least populated of all the states. Wyoming's government attempted to entice more to come with promises of jobs in ranching, farming, and mining. Officials promised the state was a place of "cures for special maladies" including tuberculosis, an especially dreaded disease of the times. It wasn't.

As with other groups of immigrants, the Finns generally settled near one another in what were called "Finntowns." Another name for their settlements was "pesäpaikka," or "nesting place." One pesäpaikka was Kenilworth, Utah. Another was Diamondville, Wyoming.

> *"Among the materials that are dug because they are useful," the ancient Greek scientist Theophrastus wrote around 300 B.C., "those known as coals are made of earth, and once set on fire, they burn like charcoal...used by those who work in metals."42*

Kenilworth was one of the many Rocky Mountain communities owing its existence to those rotting corpses of ancient plants. Some 70 miles southeast of Provo, it sits below a spectacular view of the mountains to the west. The historic myths claim it all began when a man on a horse discovered an outcropping of coal along the barren plain. One thing led to another and soon mining companies arrived, coal was being mined and transported elsewhere, out-of-state businessmen were getting rich, and miners were being exploited.[43]

It's not clear when Matti and Karolina set up house in Kenilworth but Nestori, later to be called Nestor, their second-to-the-youngest of four children, was born there on November 9, 1903. He was baptized a week later, according to a Baptismal Certificate, "in the name of God, the Father, Son, and Holy Spirit." Matti went to work for the Independent Coal and Coke Company, a Wyoming corporation, employing 40 miners working the Utah mines, tipples, and coke ovens on the site that became the township known as Kenilworth. When Matti and Karolina came, there were about 500 residents. The town never had more than 1100.

Matti and his fellow miners wore wooden shoes with slots on the soles that fit over the rails, permitting them to ski quickly down the iron rails that were laid on the mountainside. The company store was the only place they and their families could shop for groceries and other items, a benefit more to the company than the miners because prices at company stores were high and purchases deducted from paychecks. It was common that at the end of the month, the miner owed the company more than the pay the miner earned with his hard work.

Matti and Karolina undoubtedly began raising their newborns in one of the tents the company provided for its employees until boarding houses were built in 1908. By 1920, the Mottonens moved into a four-room bungalow below a hill where the company executives lived in what the miners sarcastically called "Silk-Stocking Row."

A Greek coffee house and a Boy Scout hall soon joined the saloon and the company store as the new town grew. As with many of these company towns, a schoolhouse was last in line. The classrooms were overflowing but classroom size was reduced when many of the boys left school to go to work alongside their fathers. Among them was Nestor. Sixteen short years after his birth, Nestor donned his wooden shoes and followed his father into the mines in spite of the poet William Keating's turn-of-the-century warning:

> When I was a boy says my daddy to me,
> "Stay out of the mines, take my warning," says he,
> "Or with dust you'll be choked and a pauper you'll be,
> Broken down, broken down.[44]

Two hundred twenty miles north of Kenilworth, Andrew and Hilma Matson started their Wyoming life in another coal mining community. In the late 1800s, Diamondville was nothing more than a town of shacks and dugouts built along a hillside near the coal mine where Andrew went to work. The town acquired its name from the diamond-like shine on the coal underneath the town. Before J.C. Penney decided Kemmerer, Wyoming would be the site of his first store, he scouted out Diamondville. According to a brief history of the commercial enterprise we know as J.C. Penney, an article in the Spring 2008 "Annals of Wyoming" quoted Mr.

Penney as having said of Diamondville, "I'd never been there but in Evanston (Wyoming), I'd waited on Diamondville folks. I knew their kind. They were my kind." His partners weren't impressed with the small mining town and ultimately, they all agreed the first J.C. Penney store would open down the road a mile and a half in Kemmerer.

Diamondville had but a single purpose. It housed miners and their families like Andrew and Hilma who became man and wife in 1895. He was 24. Hilma was 18. Diamondville was home.

Andrew would have been safer if he'd gone to work driving cattle or building the railroad. Mining has always been a particularly hazardous occupation, more so in the late 1800s and early 1900s. It was unlawful for women to work in the mines. Boys had to be at least 15 years old to go under the ground to dig up coal. The state employed a mine inspector as the Wyoming Constitution required. My father talked of how the inspectors always called ahead to warn the mine managers of their pending arrival at the mines where he worked. It would have been no different at the mines where Andrew worked. There was much more concern for what was brought out of the ground than the people who brought it out.

The attitude mine owners demonstrated was not unlike the 19th century Georgia plantation owner who was asked why he used Irishmen and not his African-born slaves to clear the swamp. "It's dangerous work," he replied, "and a negro's (sic) life is too valuable to be risked at it. If a negro (sic) dies, it's a considerable loss, you know."[45] Immigrant coal miners, Finnish, Irish, and so many other lives had little value to the mine owners. The mines were especially dangerous for those who came from parts of the world like Finland, where industrialization was at best in its infancy. Nearly nine out of ten fatal mining incidents involved immigrants. In one year, 1900, twenty-four miners died. "Immigrants were more likely than native miners to face injury because their bosses used a language they didn't understand."[46] The deaths "primarily befell Finnish immigrants."[47] Often as not, the state coal inspector found no one to blame.

There were no genuine safety protections in place and fatalities were commonplace in a business culture that saw fatalities as a fatalistic part of the industry and blamed the miners. Poignantly, many of the miners came to Diamondville after three separate

Andrew and Hilma Matson not long after they emigrated to the United States from Finland.

fatal explosions in Almy, Wyoming caused owners to reluctantly conclude coal could not be safely mined there. The mines there were closed and the workers were relocated.[48]

Andrew and Hilma were Scandinavian Lutherans. Back home in Perho, Finland, Andrew dutifully took the reins, guiding the Lutheran minister's horse and buggy as the cleric made home visits. Andrew waited in the cold, huddling for warmth in the buggy while the minister went inside a parishioner's warm home for a pastoral visit. Now in Diamondville there were no houses of worship dedicated to Lutherans. The only churches in town belonged to the Methodists and the Mormons. There was also a one-room schoolhouse and a mercantile. There were immigrants from many nations. There were Finns enough to open Finn Hall for the cultural celebrations that took place there regularly.

Finn Hall was where people gathered on February 26, 1901 to mourn the loss of 50 miners in a fire and explosion at Mine No. 1 at Diamondville. Many of those were Finns. Mining accidents produced trauma throughout the community as families waited hours or days to learn what had happened and to whom it had happened. At Finn Hall some women learned on that cold wintery day that they were now widows while others, including Hilma, consoled them while silently giving thanks it was not their husband on the list. The *Deseret News*, February 28, 1901, described the horror as men, women, and children waited for news about loved ones.

> *"Leaning against the baggage car which contains a score of coffins sent by Undertaker S. D. Evans, of Salt Lake, all day long there has been a knot of sober faced men and grief-stricken women, silent and woebegone. Some of the women bear traces of their headlong flight toward the scene of the horror of the night previous, as an occasional bandaged head testifies in mute testimony to the blind stumbling in the dark over the railroad tracks, through the mud, slush and rivulets of water that abound on all sides."*

When all were accounted for, it was learned that most of the deceased were Finns, Italians, and Austrians. This wasn't the first time Andrew and Hilma and the others went through this pain and it wouldn't be the last. The following October another mine disaster claimed more lives, four years later yet more. The *San Francisco Call* of February 3, 1905, said the explosion's shock resounded throughout the town, "rocking buildings so violently that their occupants ran out into the open." But the mine's owners reopened the hole a week later, not long enough after the dead were buried.

In December, there was yet another. The *Rock Springs Independent* called it "The Diamondville Horror."[49] The newspaper's report was grim. "Never has so sad a Sunday ever visited Diamondville." The *Independent* said, "Even the snow-clad hills surrounding the little town glistened pity." There was, they said, "no need to hurry" for the rescue. All the men died instantly 4,000 feet below the mouth of the mine. "White faced widows and half a dozen orphans are all that remain of those stalwart giants upon whom they leaned and to whom they looked for love and protection."

By then, it was not only Hilma who depended on Andrew. Cecelia was born in Diamondville on March 19, 1903. They soon left Diamondville. By the 1920s, the Matsons and the Mottonens and their children Nestor and Cecelia became a part of the large Finnish Community of Rock Springs.

39   *Finns in the United States,* Edited by Auvo Kostiainen, East Lansing-Michigan State University Press (2014), 41.

40   A. Dudley Gardner and Verla R. Flores, *Forgotten Frontier-A History of Wyoming Coal Mining,* Boulder, San Francisco and London-Westview Press (1989), 62.

41   Gardner, *Forgotten Frontier,* 64.

42   Chamois L. Andersen, "The Coal Business in Wyoming," WyoHistory. org, http://www.wyohistory.org/encyclopedia/coal-business-wyoming, accessed January 12, 1917.

43   Much of the history of Kenilworth was found at http://www.carbon-utgenweb.com/story.html

44   William Keating in George Korson's *"Minstrels of the Mine Patch"* University of Pennsylvania Press-Philadelphia (1938), 48.

45 Ronald Takaki, *A Different Mirror: A History of Multicultural America,* Back Bay Books (1993), 151.

46 Marilyn Nesbit Wood, *The Day the Whistle Blew: Life and Death of the Stansbury Coal Camp,* High Plains Press (2014), 46.

47 *Forgotten Frontier,* Supra., 86

48 Much of the information about Diamondville is found in "Historic Diamondville" diamondvillewyo.com/history.htm, wyomingtalesandtrails.com/coal3a.html, and www.uwyo.edu/robertshistory/coal_safety_07.htm, Accessed August 31, 2016

49 Wyoming Newspaper Project, *Rock Springs Independent,* December 8, 2905, 3, http://pluto.wyo.gov/awweb/main.jsp?flag=browse&smd=2&awdid=3, Accessed September 2, 2016

CHAPTER FOUR

AND WHEN YOU GET TO ROCK SPRINGS, YOU STAY
AWAY FROM THE COOLIES. THE FINNS IS OKAY IF
THEY AREN'T DRINKING

When the Matsons and Mottonens came to Sweetwater County, they found themselves in an environment very different from home. The treeless, bleak desert landscape of that part of Wyoming coupled with long cold winters and relentless summer heat was made even more long-suffering by the social isolation.

At times in those early days, the Finns received less than an "open-arms" welcome in Rock Springs. In his historical novel centered on the Chinese Massacre in Rock Springs, Brian Leung imagines a young woman from back East traveling by train to join her brother homesteading in Sweetwater County. An older woman takes the seat next to her and offers some advice on how to stay safe in the Wyoming territory. "And when you get to Rock Springs, you stay away from the coolies. The Finns is okay if they aren't drinking, but the coolies are the most savage lot you'll ever meet."[50]

Soon there were miners from at least 32 different nations working the Sweetwater County mines. Foreign-born employees outnumbered U.S. workers more than two to one. Over time the melting-pot effect brought down most of the barriers. Rock Springs' identity seems to have always centered on the idea that the coming together of people from a variety or ethnicities and cultures makes ours better. I grew up in a community where differences didn't matter. It wasn't a question of tolerance. It was a matter of having little or no awareness of the differences. Character mattered. Skin color or ethnic background didn't. The culture of others was celebrated by the community. The festivals and holidays of the Old World were a part of the new life in the community, enjoyed by all. I don't think I ever heard anyone complain upon hearing a language other than English being spoken. No one ever told someone else to "Go back home." But, that was the 1930s and 40s. The acceptance was hard earned in battles fought in earlier days.

Even so, the old woman's admonition about Finns and "coolies" was consistent with some of the resentment felt among U.S. born miners toward immigrants in general and Finns and Chinese workers in particular. In 1886, not long before Andrew arrived, one Union Pacific official said the company preferred to recruit Finnish immigrants to work their Wyoming mines, adding to the resentment.

The Finns exhibited characteristics the mine bosses appreciated in addition to their ability to work hard and be dependable employees. Tarja Moles wrote a humorous expose of Finnish characteristics titled *A Xenophobe's Guide to the Finns.* "A Finn can get extremely angry or ecstatically happy without the use of any facial expressions or change of tone of voice. He will only wave his hands if drowning."[51] The Finns, she says, "don't see the point of small talk." If you ask one "how are you?" he or she will think you actually want to know. A Finnish word explains their nature. To exhibit *Sisu* is to be characterized by stamina, doggedness, and tenacity. It also explains their independence. *Sisu* may also explain why they "didn't fraternize with other miners" and weren't inclined to join the unions that gave UP management such a hard time. It was this reputation that led other miners to resent the Finns. One miner targeted Finns with this complaint. "A practical miner comes along and applies for work and he is refused, a Finnlander comes right after him and gets the work."[52]

An 1893 labor dispute defied the Finn's reputation for complacency. One night, more than 200 Finns, having been ignored in their concerns about a certain difficult mine boss, marched on the company office. They gave the "boss twenty-four hours to leave the camp. If found after that time, they would hang him." The boss, unwilling to rely on the Finn's reputation for complacency, left *post haste.*[53]

Trains like that on which the young easterner traveled west in Leung's historic fiction were foundational to the history of Rock Springs and Wyoming. Those trains were the reason so much coal could be mined in Wyoming. Before the railroad, mines were small, serving only local customers needing the coal to heat their homes and businesses. Farmers bartered their eggs, crops, and meat for a wagonload of coal. Once the transcontinental rail was laid and train cars became widely available, the Union Pacific created a massive national and international marketing system connecting "sources of revenue, such as mines, mills, factories, and farms, with markets where products could be sold and income from freight received."[54]

A DAY OF VIOLENCE AND BLACK INJUSTICE

In 1888, the year before Andrew Matson arrived in the U.S., 1501 men were employed in Union Pacific's Wyoming mines. By the time Andrew had been here but a year that number more than doubled to 3,564. Coal production tripled in the decade ending in 1890, the year Wyoming became a state.[55] A 1940 history of the coal mines of the Union Pacific Railroad is dedicated to "the memory of the men and women who, putting all else behind them, made their full contribution toward translating an endless area of mountain, desert, and plain into the empire now known as 'the West." Andrew Matson, Matti and Nestor Mottonen were three of those men.

Andrew left Finland and joined hundreds of his fellow countrymen in the employ of the Union Pacific in 1891. When he went to work for UP in Rock Springs, the Chinese Massacre was still a fresh memory. The anonymous writers of the *History of the Union Pacific Coal Mines* called September 2, 1885, "a day of violence and black injustice, when the blood of innocent men soaked (Rock Springs) soil and the stench of burning flesh arose from smoking ruins."[56] Just as labor strife between the Union Pacific and its American employees resulted in the mining company soliciting foreign workers, including those Finns who came before Andrew Matson, it was the 1875 strike that caused the company to import Chinese labor.

The infamous event that many Wyomingites would just as soon forget began in the fall of 1875 as a labor dispute between UP and the Knights of Labor. The Knights had, by then, become a powerful force in labor relations. With more than 700,000 members, the union demanded an eight-hour workday, the end of child labor, and fair pay. So, the union's anger could have been predicted when the Union Pacific asked members to increase coal production by twenty-five percent without a corresponding wage hike. The Knights refused. Union Pacific's strategy, in response, was to pit worker against worker. Then, as now, it was easy to scapegoat those who are different. The company's president notified the Knights that, "in a short time I will have a body of men here who will dig for us all the coal we want." Two months later, 300 Chinese workers arrived in Rock Springs and began digging coal.[57] The Union members' response was a strike. The company then fired many of them. Resentments among remaining white miners built for a decade before the September 1885 explosion.

John L. Lewis was the president of the United Mine Workers and represented most of the white miners who weren't members of the Knights. Lewis protested to Beckwith, Quinn and Company, the organization under contract with UP to supply the Chinese labor force. Lewis knew what was ahead and tried to persuade the company to take action to avoid it. "It pains me greatly to call your attention to the fact that the Chinese problem at Rock Springs is assuming a grave attitude. Was it not for the fact that I am sensible, I would not trouble you with correspondence upon the matter."

Lewis then added an ominous prediction. "Sensible as I am, unless a change is effected immediately there will be an outbreak. I respectfully notify you of the storm that is brewing."[58] On August 28, 1885, the UMW president followed up with a letter to the head of Union Pacific, D.O. Clark. "For God's sake," Lewis wrote, "do what you can to avoid this calamity." Lewis's union members didn't give Clark enough time.

Chinese miners came to the U.S. as early as 1849 to mine gold during the California Gold Rush.[59] Later many were hired to build the transcontinental railroad. Ten percent of the 12,000 Chinese workers doing the dangerous tasks of blasting hard rock to clear tunnels were killed before the rail lines were completed. When these jobs disappeared, many of the Chinese workers looked to mining for employment.

Wyoming historian Tom Rea described their living conditions. "The whites—mostly Irish, Scandinavian, English and Welsh immigrants—lived in downtown Rock Springs. The Chinese lived in what the whites called Chinatown, to the northeast, on the other side of a bend in the railroad tracks and across Bitter Creek." For several years they worked side by side but language and cultural differences assured there was no assimilation. The Chinese were willing to work for low wages, which kept all workers' wages down. The result was continued conflict between the union and Union Pacific. An 1884 strike was the last straw. Mine managers were ordered to hire only Chinese workers.

The resentments turned violent on the morning of September 2, 1885. One Chinese worker was killed and another severely wounded in a fight near the Number 6 mine in Rock Springs. A Union Pacific foreman ordered an end to that fight but the angry white miners went home and gathered knives, guns, and anything they could use for clubs. They gathered at a saloon where anger mixed with alcohol. The mob then marched to "Chinatown" where they dragged Chinese people from their homes, beating them and killing many while looting and burning their dwellings.

Twenty-eight Chinese lost their lives but no eye witnesses other than the Chinese victims, whom the jury was not inclined to believe, could be found to testify about what happened and who did the killing. No charges were ever filed after the Grand Jury, which the authors of the *History of the Union Pacific Coal Mines* called "anti-Chinese," concluded, "Whatever crimes may have been committed there on the 2nd of September, the perpetrators thereof have not been disclosed by the evidence before us." Nonetheless, the Grand Jury report did fault the Union Pacific.

> *"While we find no excuse for the crimes committed, there appears to be no doubt abuses existed that should have been promptly adjusted by the railroad*

*company and its officers. If this had been done the fair
name of our Territory would not have been stained by
the terrible events of the 2nd of September."* [60]

Surviving Chinese workers demanded to be provided a train to leave. Union Pacific officials "tricked" them into boarding a train, telling them it would take them to San Francisco. It went as far as Evanston, Wyoming, about 100 miles away, where in the night it turned around and headed back to Rock Springs. The safety of these men was of secondary concern. The UP needed the Chinese to bury their dead, rebuild their shacks, and continue mining.

The federal troops that Governor Francis Warren requested be sent to Rock Springs to control the violence were still there when Andrew Matson came to Wyoming in 1891. By the time Andrew arrived in Rock Springs in the 1920s, the relationship between the Chinese and white communities had improved greatly. Each shared in the customs and celebrations of the other. The Rock Springs at which Andrew arrived had an array of bars and saloons, a brewery, food markets offering fresh fish and oysters, at least two opera houses including the "Conried Opera Company" and "Edgars' Opera House." The education of the community's

Chinese Massacre. Wyoming - Rock Springs
Photo courtesy of the American Heritage Center, University of Wyoming

children was valued enough that the *Rock Springs Miner* printed a monthly report on school progress informing folks the number of students enrolled in each grade, how many were tardy or absent that month, and named the "pupils whose general average was 85 percent or over."[61]

The newspapers reported that, by then, many who had pioneered Sweetwater County and Wyoming were dying off. Auntie Davis was one such pioneer. She came to Sweetwater County in the mid-1880s around the time of the first documented mention of the coal that Lois's grandfathers and father would spend a career mining. Even today the expanse and desolation of the Red Desert separating towns in Sweetwater County, raises the question of how people like Auntie Davis could have made a life on that part of the planet. But they did, and proudly. Another such pioneer was Elinore Pruitt Stewart.

ON EVERY SIDE OF US STRETCHED THE POOR, HELPLESS DESERT

Elinore Pruitt Stewart came a few years later than Auntie Davis but not much had changed in the intervening years. Stewart wrote a popular book about her life on that land, "Letters of a Woman Homesteader."[62] She arrived to homestead on the Wyoming side of the Utah border in the spring of 1909, after twenty-four hours on a train and two days on a stage coach. There was then fifteen feet of snow on her land. As it melted, Stewart found sagebrush "so short in some places that it is not large enough to make a fire." She then described the scenery that must have caused others to stay.

> *"After driving all day over what seemed a level desert of sand, we came about sundown to a beautiful cañón, down which we had to drive a couple of miles before we could cross. In the cañón the shadows had already fallen, but when looked up we could see the last shafts of sunlight on the tops of the great bare buttes. After we quitted the cañón, I saw the most beautiful sight.*

It seemed as if we were driving through a golden haze.
The violet shadows were creeping up between the hills,
while away back of us the snow-capped peaks were
catching the sun's last rays. On every side of us stretched
the poor, helpless desert, the sage grim and determined
to live in spite of starvation and the great, bare, desolate
buttes. The beautiful colors turned to amber and rose,
and then to the general tone, dull gray."[63]

People came and many still come to make a living, often from mining or related industry and businesses. Though making a living can be a challenge, they stay for the same reason Elinor Pruitt Stewart stayed.

Despite the harshness of the environment, those who stay eventually figure out how to make a life there. The oldest living person in Wyoming died as the Mottonens were finding a life in Rock Springs. James "Dad" Sherrod was 104 years old. In his venturous lifetime, he had driven stagecoaches and fought Indians. "He was present," the newspaper reported, "at the Thornberg (sic) massacre and was one of the defenders at the white colony in that desperate battle against the redmen (sic)."[64]

In 1920, the so-called Indian Wars were fresh on the minds of the old-timers. Fewer than two generations had come and gone since the battle in which Mr. Sherrod had fought, not long enough for American history to have caught up with the facts. The Thornburgh Massacre was the culmination of a scheme to drive the Ute Indians out of Colorado and make vast amounts of land available to rich white men. William B. Vickers, a Denver newspaper editor and politician "began drumming up a propaganda campaign to have all the Utes exiled to Indian Territory, thus leaving an immense amount of valuable land free for the taking." Vickers described the plot in a *Denver Tribune* article:

> *"The Utes are actual, practical Communists and*
> *the government should be ashamed to foster and*
> *encourage them in their idleness and wanton waste*

*of property." Vickers described how Nathan C. Meeker
had gone to the White River Agency as Superintendent
with high hopes to reform the Indian lifestyle.
"But utter failure marked his efforts and at last he
reluctantly accepted the truth of the border truism
that the only truly good Indians are dead ones."*[65]

Meeker's steadfast inability to be honest about the Utes with
whose care he was charged eventually led Washington to order
Major Thomas T. "Tip" Thornburgh to march his troops from Ft.
Steele, near Rawlins, Wyoming to confront the Utes at Mill Creek
in Northern Colorado. Though the Utes made several attempts to
demonstrate that Meeker's reports of their hostilities were false,
"Thornburgh succumbed to a harebrained, deceitful scheme by his
second in command" and put his troops in a position interpreted
by the Utes to be warlike.[66] The fighting lasted nearly a week and
left Major Thornburgh and 12 of his men dead. Nathan Meeker
was killed, "a bullet hole in his head and a logging chain wrapped
around his neck. The Utes had clubbed his skull and pounded a
metal stake down his throat. He would tell no more lies."[67] Among
the Utes, thirty-seven "died in what they believed was a desperate
stand to save their reservation from military seizure..."[68] It was,
however futile. More soldiers came and soon "Colorado was swept
clean of Indians. Cheyenne and Arapaho, Kiowa and Comanche,
Jicarilla and Ute, they had all known its mountains and plains, but
now no trace of them remained but their names on the white man's
land."[69]

But in 1920, the Sweetwater County newspaper was still
celebrating all of that with an article heralding James "Dad"
Sherrod's military service while ironically betraying how little care
was given military veterans even in that day. After surviving the
Indian campaigns of the 19th century, "Sherrod died," reported the
Rock Springs Miner, "in a poor farm in Carbon County after living
an early Wyoming life symbolic of the whites who came to settle
the west." The way in which the nation treats those who fight its
wars has a long, sordid history.

A GREEK BAKER, A CHINESE RESTAURANT,
AND A JEWISH MARKET

By the 1920s, the Indian Wars were in the past. Rock Springs was now a melting pot of cultures. The Chinese Massacre demonstrated how difficult the assimilation process was but by the 1920s, "the town began celebrating its diversity with 'International Night,' a festival that showcased cultural differences by sharing food, songs, and dance." Japanese descendants appeared in traditional dress as did Scottish, Italian, German, and Finnish families. The celebration included a ceremony in which people from each nation lighted a candle to represent their heritage until all candles burned together as a symbol of their shared American life. The tradition continues today.[70]

In the early days, non-native born residents outnumbered those born in the United States. There were Italians, Slavs, Greeks, Mexicans, Germans, Czechs, Austrians, Danes, French, Hungarians, Japanese, Chinese, Irish, Swedes, Scotts, Russians and, of course Finns among others. Places like Finn Hall and Slovenski Dome assured the old-world customs were honored by people who were a part of the Rock Springs community. The Rock Springs of that day could teach the U.S. of today a great deal about the ability of people from different backgrounds to live together. Diversity was such an obvious and celebrated community trait that many years later, Thomas Cullen, a longtime resident remembered one street that housed "a Greek baker, a Chinese restaurant, and a Jewish market."[71] Slovenian immigrants sold baked goods including baklava on Pilot Butte Avenue. Barbers, leather craftsmen, shoe repair shops, tailors, gas stations and tire repair shops joined the many saloons where immigrants could go to hear their language spoken.

Mostly though, Rock Springs was a mining town. George Baxter, who served as Territorial Governor for 30 days in 1886, toasted Sweetwater County in 1892, telling an audience, "as for our coal, we believe we have it in sufficient quantities to keep the furnace fires of the world burning for a thousand years."[72] Today the coal companies like to deny they are at the root of threatening changes in the planet's climate. They hire faux scientists to spew questionable claims that they are not. However, an August 14, 1912, an article in *The Rodmen and Omaha Times* admitted,

> *"The furnaces of the world are now burning about 2,000,000,000 tons of coal a year. When this is burned, uniting with oxygen, it adds about 7,000,000,000 tons of carbon dioxide to the atmosphere yearly. This tends to make the air a more effective blanket for the earth and to raise its temperature. The effect may be considerable in a few centuries."*

Here we are more than a century later and still electing Wyoming politicians who refuse to hear what competent, honest scientists have been telling us for decades.

The increasing coal production at the turn of the 19th century was heralded by the press and the politicians. It may have been good for those corporations that owned the mines but they shared very little of the wealth with those who actually produced the wealth. Making matters worse, low wages for miners were coupled with post World War I inflation causing the cost of living to rise significantly. Food costs soared by 94% since pre-war levels and clothing by more than 135%.[73]

Lois's parents Nestor and Cecelia

The son of Italian immigrants, Celeste Roncaglio, was born in Rock Springs in the 1920s. He grew up poor there as did so many, shining shoes and carrying a sandwich sign board to help his family get by during the Depression years. Like many others, Roncaglio took what he learned on the streets of that culturally-diverse community and made good. Teno Roncalio, as he came to be known, won a Silver Star in World War II and returned home to become a successful attorney and banker before serving a decade in the U.S. House of Representatives. His successes in later life epitomized the best of Rock Springs while his early life there epitomized how tough a place it was in the 20s. It was like that for many of those who were raised in Rock Springs including myself.

In 1927, Cecelia and Nestor went to see the Justice of the Peace in Green River, the Sweetwater County seat. There they married and drove back to Rock Springs afterward to celebrate at Finn Hall. After the wedding, Nestor continued pounding away in the coal mines. Cecelia spent her time between two jobs as a seamstress in two tailor shops. Before their wedding, Cecelia had taken cosmetology courses in Salt Lake City.

Lois Carolin Mottonen was born at the Rock Springs general hospital on May 14, 1929. She weighed 6 pounds 8 ounces.

TEXAS WAS EMOTIONAL;
WYOMING WAS CHIVALRIC

I missed it but had I been born a few years earlier I'd have been a witness to the last time Wyoming did anything to lay claim to its grand claim to be the "Equality State." In 1924, Wyoming elected a person who would become the first woman to be sworn into the office of Governor in any state.

Here's how that happened. On October 2, 1924, Nellie became a widow when her husband died after an appendicitis attack. William Bradford Ross, a Democrat, was nearly two years into a four-year term as Wyoming's Governor. There would be a special election on 5th. The Democrats quickly nominated the deceased Governor's widow.

Coincidentally, a woman was also seeking the Governorship of Texas at this very same time. Miriam "Ma" Ferguson was the favorite in that contest. It is to Ma Ferguson that history attributes, or as some argue mis-attributes, a classic quote. As the Governor, she was, they say, incensed to learn that Spanish was being spoken in public schools. 'If English was good enough for Jesus Christ, then it's good enough for Texas." Her campaign slogan was, "Me for Ma and I ain't got a durned thing against Pa."

As Election Day 1924 approached it was more certain that Texas, not Wyoming, was going to elect a female Governor. Under Wyoming law, however, the first woman ever sworn in to a Governorship would be Nellie Tayloe Ross, if the Democrat could overcome the state's large Republican majority and win the election. Mrs. Ross slogan became, "Beat Texas to it."[74] And Wyoming did. With the two females vying for the Governorship of their respective states, some were able to understand what was happening only in terms of emotionalism and chivalry. The *Denver Republican* used this headline to explain the election results in both states, "Texas was emotional; Wyoming was chivalric."[75] Nellie Tayloe Ross won a huge majority, defeating her GOP opponent by 8,000 votes when 79,000 voted. Mrs. Ross was sworn into the office of Governor of Wyoming 20 days before Ma Ferguson was sworn into the office of Governor of Texas.

Just as the 2nd Territorial Legislature tried valiantly to undo the law passed by the 1st Territorial Legislature granting suffrage to women, there were a lot of Wyoming men who couldn't wait until Mrs. Ross stood for reelection two years later to return a man to that office. Mrs. Ross herself didn't seem to believe politics to be a woman's highest calling. "I am old fashioned enough," she said, "to believe that no career is as glorious as that which wifehood and motherhood offer."[76] Even so, Nellie was willing to challenge the idea of political patriarchy. "Let no one suppose," she said in one campaign speech, "that the perils and hardships (of building the state) were endured only by men."[77]

It was one thing to give the last two years of a dead man's term in office to his widow; it was quite another to give her a four-year term in her own right. Governor Ross lost a close reelection fight in November 1928 by a slim 1,365 votes out of more than 70,000 votes cast. A Denver newspaper blamed it on two factors; one was the large Wyoming Republican majority; the other, "an undercurrent of prejudice among some citizens against the participation of women in political affairs, and the argument was commonly made during the campaign that no woman, however able should be allowed to serve as Governor."[78]

Indeed, since Nellie Tayloe Ross served those two years, "no woman, however able" has ever been allowed to serve as Governor of Wyoming. Three tried. Wyoming voters elected Mary Mead's father Cliff Hansen for Governor before she ran and her son Matt Mead afterward in 2010, but rejected her in 1990. The voters handily elected Kathy Karpan to be Secretary of State twice. Kathy

FOR GOVERNOR

MRS. NELLIE TAYLOE ROSS
Able, Qualified, Independent
She Has No Interest but the Interests of the State

Nellie Tayloe Ross campaign picture
Photo courtesy of the American Heritage Center, University of Wyoming

could likely have remained in that office forever even though she was a Democrat. But the voters of Wyoming said "nope" when she tried to become Governor in 1994. Rita Meyer was a highly qualified business person and high-ranking National Guard officer but couldn't get by a 2010 GOP primary. Wyoming young people have grown up being taught with pride about Nellie Tayloe Ross. Governor Matt Mead's wife continued the propaganda with her recent book called "Wyoming Firsts." It also touts the results of that 1926 election as something uniquely special about the state. Wyoming has been a state for more than a century and a quarter. It's had one woman Governor serve two years. That is apparently sufficient criterion for calling yourself the "Equality State."

I grew up, came of age, and worked in a state to which the motto no longer told the truth.

50   Brian Leung, *Take Me Home,*" Harper Collins Publishers (2010), 29

51   Tarja Moles, *A Xenophobe's Guide to the Finns,* published by Xenophobe's Guides (2011), 1

52   Gardner, *Forgotten Frontier,* Supra., 83.

53   Gardner, *Forgotten Frontier,* 88

54   Gardner, *Forgotten Frontier,* 65

55   Gardner, *Forgotten Frontier,* 61

56   Anonymous Authors, *History of the Union Pacific Coal Mines,* The Colonial Press-Omaha Nebraska (1940), 75.

57   *History of the Union Pacific Coal Mines,* 76

58   *History of the Union Pacific Coal Mines,* 79

59   Tom Rea, "The Rock Springs Massacre, http://www.wyohistory.org/essays/rock-springs-massacre, accessed July 20, 2016 (unless otherwise noted the description of the Chinese Massacre are taken from Mr. Rea's account).

60   *History of the Union Pacific Coal Mines,* 89.

61   "Monthly Report," *Rock Springs Miner,* February 10, 1892, 3.

62   "Elinore Pruitt Stewart, *Letters of a Woman Homesteader,* A Mariner Book-Houghton Mifflin Company-Boston and New York (Originally copyrighted 1913).

63   Id., 9,10

64   *Rock Springs Miner,* January 2, 1920, 4.

65   Dee Brown, *Bury My Heart at Wounded Knee,* Picador-Henry Holt and Company-New York (1970), 376.

66   Peter Cozzens, *The Earth is Weeping-The Epic Story of the Indian Wars for the*

American West. Alfred A. Knopf-New York (2016), 352.

67   Cozzens, *The Earth is Weeping*, 353.

68   Brown, *Bury My Heart*, 387.

69   Brown, *Bury My Heart*, 389

70   Russel L. Tanner and Margie Fletcher Shanks, *Rock Springs-Images of America,* Arcadia Publishing (2008).

71   "Rock Springs, Wyoming" by Chris Probst, www.wyohistory.org/essays/rock-springs-wyoming, Accessed November 16, 2016.

72   "Discourses Upon Wyoming's Future," *Rock Springs Miner,* February 17, 1892, 1.

73   *Rock Springs Miner,* January 09, 1920, 5.

74   Undated manuscript, File: "Speeches and Notes" Box 7, Folder 13, Papers of Nellie Tayloe Ross, Accession No. 948-97-10-07, American Heritage Center, University of Wyoming (NTR Papers).

75   Undated 1926 clipping, Box 22, Scrapbook, NTR Papers

76   Manuscript of Nellie Tayloe Ross speech, March 28, 1928, Box 23, Scrapbook, NTR Papers.

77   Undated manuscript, File: "Speeches and Notes" Box 7, Folder 13, NTR Papers.

78   Undated manuscript, File: "Speeches and Notes" Box 7, Folder 13, NTR Paper

CHAPTER FIVE

WE CAN SEE WYOMING'S MOUNTAINS GIVING UP
THE HIDDEN STORES. TONS ON TONS, BY MILLIONS
POURING, OF THE BASE AND PRECIOUS ORES.[79]

My earliest memories come not from the first few years in Rock Springs, but rather the year my family spent a few miles north in Winton where my father went to work in that mine.

Winton started as a coal camp for Megeath Coal Company in 1917, but became a Union Pacific company town four years later. Leaving Rock Springs and heading north, you climb about 1500 feet over just 14 miles before arriving at Winton, 7,000 feet above sea level. A Union Pacific authorized history of the company's Wyoming mining operations includes a chapter ironically titled, "Winton, the Town That Will Live on For Years."[80] Winton lived little more than a decade after the book was published.

Annie Proulx reminds us that neither Megeath nor the Union Pacific was the first to come to Winton. The first humans came to the region surrounding Winton, what we call the Red Desert, 12,000 years before the mining companies.[81] They didn't stay long, but more came as the west was settled in the 19th century. Only a handful of the 350,000 pioneers who traveled through the area in wagon trains stayed to ranch or mine. Nothing human ever stayed long near Winton.

The mining industry has a long history of creating ghost towns. Great promises and hope give way to abandonment. The mining companies always, then as now, blame government policy. But, the truth is that ghost towns are an inherent part of the business plan in a coal-based economy. The company finds the coal and brings miners and their families to the site. A town appears with a company store at its center. They pay those miners a pittance to dig it up and haul it away until the price of coal falls to where that is no longer economically feasible. The cycle ends, often abruptly at least from the perspective of the miners who are always the last to know. The company moves down the road to the next future ghost town with little regard for the damage done to families.

Today Winton is one of Wyoming's many ghost towns that began as mining communities. Though no viable structures remain, there are thick concrete foundations announcing that there was once a large company store, administration building, a bath house, the tipple, and the track on which trains came to be loaded with coal, traces of which can still be seen along the ground. Anyone with a vivid imagination can see there was once also a school, a mule barn, doctor's office, post office, show hall, and a pool hall. There were Catholic and Mormon churches. The concrete foundation outlines left among the sand dunes at Winton are now filled with broken beer and whiskey bottles used by someone for target practice after they had emptied them. Now there is no trace of the school, the miners' boardinghouse, clapboard homes or outhouses. Their wooden structures were long ago torn down and carted off for other uses by other people in

Winton, Wyoming in winter.

other places. The schoolhouse was dismantled and reconstructed as a saloon somewhere near the Utah border. The mine office was sent off to become a cabin somewhere around Pinedale. Another building became the American Legion Hall at Fort Bridger.[82]

TURNED A ROCKY KNOLL INTO
A BEAUTIFUL GARDEN

If you listen with your imagination, you may hear that which was long ago carried away in the Wyoming wind as it blew across Winton. It's the sounds of the eight languages spoken when as many as 700 immigrant miners worked the three coal mines at Winton.

But, when I was a four-year old, Winton was the center of my life. Father worked those Winton mines and my mother kept house there. Our house was near the mine entrance. The walls had no insulation. I can still see the dirt and coal dust making its way through the cracks, which allowed me to watch passersby. There were wires dangerously running along the ceiling providing us with enough electricity to fire a single light bulb for the brightly colored wooden-box design structures. It never happened in our house fortunately, but fires were commonplace in other homes when housewives used gasoline to clean their husband's coal stained work clothes. Occasionally these fires took other houses with them as they were built so closely together.

Looking back now, I can see how my family was unique in that I was the only child. Many families had many children. The number of children in a family mattered not. Each house had two bedrooms, a living room and kitchen. There were no toilet facilities and no running water. Outhouses were available. Barrels of water were shipped in from Green River. However, it was sufficient for the three of us though I often wondered how the family across the street with six children made do in a house the same size.

The barrenness of the land today surrounding the ghost town differs not one bit from that surrounding the town I lived in at its thriving most in the early 1930s. The Wyoming desert sands didn't grow much but sagebrush. A popular 19th century myth held that the rain would follow the plows. It didn't, to the disappointment and ruin of many a wannabee settler.

Millions of years ago freshwater lakes were a feature of the Red Desert surrounding Winton. Fifty-two million years ago, Lake Gosiute was the geologic attribute around which much of the coal the Union Pacific coveted in 1921 was formed.[83] But by the time we Mottonens arrived, the lakes no longer existed, having dried up hundreds of centuries earlier. Today as in the 1930s, the desert around Winton might get eight inches of moisture a year and most of that comes in the form of snowflakes, which quickly blow by, leaving little moisture in the ground.

Nonetheless, many of the Winton folks found a way to grow flower and vegetable gardens along the edges of their homes. Our neighbors, Italian immigrants Frank and Mary Franch, "turned a rocky knoll into a beautiful garden."[84] Its lily pond stocked with fish was a favorite of the Winton children and the garden-contest judges. Each summer there was high competition for the most beautiful. "It was difficult for judges to pick a winner and amazing to see the wide variety of flowers and vegetables that could be grown."

We children made do as children everywhere, finding ways to entertain ourselves with one another. But for adults, Winton life was tough. Work in the mines was tough on the men. Housekeeping and child rearing was tough on their wives. You'd never guess how tough life was by glancing through the dozens of photographs in the Sweetwater County Historical Museum; old photos of hundreds of Finnish families, men in the finest suits, women in flowing dresses, babies in white gowns.[85]

HOW COULD DADDY HAVE WORKED IN A PLACE LIKE THIS?

The Union Pacific Coal Company paid a competitively low wage. When my father mined coal at Winton, the per day salary

"For White Labor" was $5.42 or less than 68 cents per hour.[86] To worsen matters, the Mottonens found themselves in Winton during the Great Depression. Families were desperate for what scarce money was to be earned. With the declining demand for coal, seasonal layoffs characterized Wyoming mining operations. The year before we arrived at Winton, Wyoming mines were in operation an average of only 145 days per year.[87] Father and the others almost never worked full 40-hour weeks. My father worked maybe two to three days a week, which didn't allow him enough pay to provide adequately for his family but proved enough time to expose him the Black Lung disease that shortened his life and made his final days much more difficult than should have been. Saturdays and Sundays were considered vacation time though he

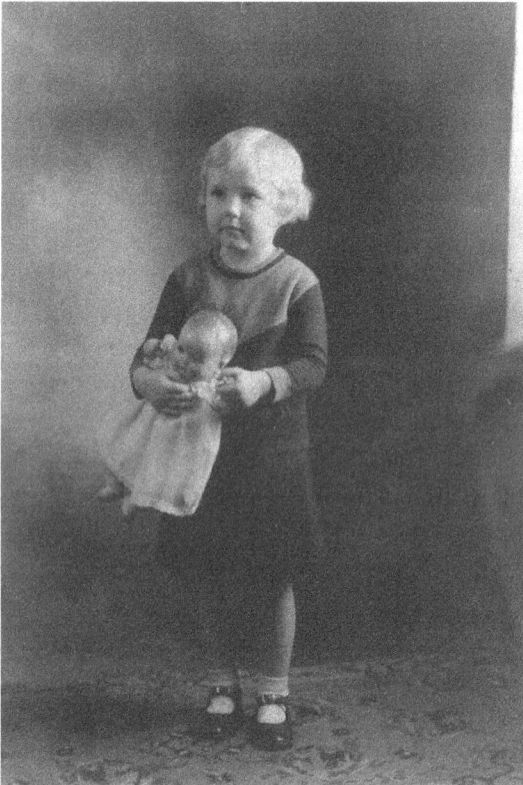

was frequently called to work weekends. The Mottonens spent a single Christmas in Winton. Money was so short that mother and father were able to give me one gift on Christmas morning along with a promise of a second gift come the next payday.

Father and his fellow miners labored in "dank, muggy air, thick with powder fumes, and no wife could be certain her man would return to her at evening with his body intact."[88] Many didn't. My mother had good reason to worry each day. She and her husband were in Diamondville when three explosions over four years widowed 68 women.[89] Neither would have known that their nationality played a role. The statistics were not good for Finns. Early 1900 Wyoming mining fatalities "primarily felled Finnish emigrants."[90] Mine inspectors generally found "no one being to blame," though it was believed that language barriers contributed to many of the accidents. In any event, there was little regulatory impetus for UP to make the mines a safer place by the time my father went to work at Winton.

Mother undoubtedly knew Marilla Caller. She had been widowed a few short years earlier when an explosion killed her husband Segundo. By now, Marilla was struggling to get by on the $40 a month she was paid to clean the mine office and whatever welfare she could find, usually in the form of surplus butter and cheese.[91] Winton wives like my mother watched Marilla and feared for their own futures. In her book "The Day the Whistle Blew," Wyoming author Marilyn Nesbit Wood tells the story of her father's death in a Sweetwater County coal mine. Years later she visited the site, now one of the Ghost towns. She asked the man who accompanied her, himself a former miner, "How could Daddy have worked in a place like this?" The answer came,

> *"You know, strange as it seems, a miner gets used to working underground. I loved it and I bet your dad did too. Farther down, it's like a city all its own where the temperature never changes. I guess it's all what you are used to. Sure, mining's dangerous. Every damn move you make is dangerous. But you just go*

to work each day hoping to hell today isn't the day the Good Lord means for you to gets yours."[92]

My father had an especially worrisome job. I am sure he went "to work each day hoping to hell today isn't the day the Good

Lois's father Nestor stands proudly in front of a coal car at Winton.

Lord" meant for him to get his. He was one of the miners who was tested and certified to prepare and set off the explosives that freed large chunks of coal far below the earth. His was among the most precarious of all the mining jobs, exposing him to an immediate risk of being injured or killed by an explosion and to the long-range risk, unknown at the time, of black lung disease. His job "involved undercutting the coal face with a hand pick. Lying on his side at arm's length from the point of dust generation, the miner could not avoid breathing mineral particles."[93] It was said that "every stroke of the pick dislodges a fresh shower of dust, to be inhaled by the miner," in this case, Nestor Mottonen.

Observers had not yet noticed, as researchers one day would, that there was a "great excess of old women over old men" in the mining communities.[94] When the iconic United Mine Workers attorney Clarence Darrow talked about the dire consequences of coal dust exposure in 1902, he did so not to improve safety, but to support a demand for increased wages. "Darrow decried a system that sentenced young children to labor in an 'everlasting cloud' of dust because of the inadequate wages paid their fathers."[95]

But father made it home each day, unaware of how that day's work would combine with all the days before in eventually ending his life. He'd stop first in the bathhouse where 30 shower stalls allowed he and the others to clean up a bit after a day below ground. A second bathhouse afforded mother and me and the other women and children a place to shower.

Cecelia awaited Nestor's return each day in a house that was far too cold in winter and suffering hot in the summer. The dirt yard was maybe not the best pace for a four-year-old to play. One afternoon, I came upon some ice cubes that had been tossed out the back door of the company store. Like any four-year-old, I picked up a handful of cubes and sucked on them and became deathly ill, falling into convulsions. My parents rushed me to Dr. Creager's office, the UP company doctor in Rock Sprigs. I recovered. No harm, no foul, as they say.

One of my Winton memories is being scared by the huge

horses ambling through town, animals that were used along with mules to haul coal from the mine to the tipple where it was then loaded on that noisy train. The "Iron Horse" passing too near their home scared me as well.

The company-owned home came at a higher-than-fair rent. The company store sold groceries at a price that made it certain the miners owed more at the end of the month than the company owed the miner. The company store here as everywhere the Union Pacific mined coal, was designed not to make life easier on the miners and their families but to "net the coal company significant profits and lead to better control of the workers."[96] The Mottonens owned a beat up old Chrysler that could sometimes make the 14-mile journey to Rock Springs where there was a new Safeway store and prices were more reasonable.

There was a school in Winton. A grade school employed five teachers for children through the eighth grade. Older children were schooled down the road at Reliance, Wyoming. Nestor Mottonen felt strongly about his daughter's education. It is a Finnish trait. Finn humorist Tarja Moles claims their success in the classroom can be attributed to Finnish weather. "If you are chucked outdoors for a quarter of an hour every 45 minutes, you're more likely to sit still at your desk when you come back inside, not only because your mind is refreshed, but because your body is too cold to do anything else."

However, father wasn't convinced the Sweetwater County cold would have the same impact on my education. He just wasn't impressed with the quality of a Winton education. So, after one long year there, Nestor packed up the family and headed back to Rock Springs so that his daughter could learn in one of Wyoming's better school districts.

79   Mrs. I.S. Bartlett, "A True Republic," Wyoming's statehood celebration on July 23, 1890, https://sites.google.com/a/wyo.gov/wyomingnewspapers/exhibit-wyoming-statehood-celebration/speeches-and-poem

80   *History of the Union Pacific Coal Mines,* Omaha-The Colonial Press (1940), 154.

81   Annie Proulx, Editor, *Red Desert: History of Place,* University of Texas Press (2008).

82   "Remembering life in Winton" by Connie Wilcox-Timar, Rocket Miner, July 18, 2010, page 4A.

83   Knight, *Mountains and Plains-The Ecology of Wyoming Landscapes, 2nd Edition,* New Haven and London-Yale University Press (2014), 15.

84   Karen Spence McLean and Marjane Telck, *Coal Camps of Sweetwater County,* Arcadia Publishing (2012), 45 (Many of the section's observations of Winton life come from this fine book, which includes an historic collection of photographs).

85   File: "Photos of Finns" Sweetwater County Historical Museum.

86   *History of the Union Pacific Coal Mines,* Appendix page xli.

87   Gardner, *Forgotten Frontier-A History of Wyoming Coal Mining,* 165.

88   *History of the Union Pacific Coal Mines,* 158.

89   Gardner, *Forgotten Frontier,* 98.

90   Gardner, *Forgotten Frontier,* 86.

91   *Coal Camps of Sweetwater County,* 47.

92   Marilyn Nesbit Wood, *"The Day the Whistle Blew,* High Plains Press (2014), 14.

93   Alan Derickson, *Black Lung-Anatomy of a Public Health Disaster,* Cornell University Press (1998), 3.

94   Derickson, *Black Lung,* 7.

95   Derickson, *Black Lung,* 37.

96   David A. Wolfe, *Industrializing the Rockies-Growth, Competition, and Turmoil in the Coalfields of Colorado and Wyoming 1868-1914,* University of Colorado Press (2003), 127.

CHAPTER SIX

FINNS REVEL IN HARDSHIP

By the time we Mottonens returned to Rock Springs from our year in Winton, the state of Wyoming was deep in the midst of the Great Depression having made it through the biggest pre-Watergate scandal in American history. Teapot Dome got its name from a look-alike rock formation in Natrona County not far from an oil field set aside as a "national petroleum reserve." It was not to be developed unless a national emergency was declared. But as they are wont to do, powerful oilmen coveted that oil. When President Warren G. Harding appointed his old card-playing buddy, U.S. Senator Albert Fall, to be the Secretary of the Interior, they had their opening.

Secretary Fall first persuaded the President to transfer jurisdiction for the national petroleum reserve from the Navy to his Interior Department. A couple of oil tycoons, including Harry Sinclair whose company bore his name, then bribed Secretary Fall into allowing them to drill the oil. The dominoes began to fall thanks to a couple of watchful Wyoming Democrats. Leslie A. Miller, then an oilman and later Wyoming's Governor, noticed "trucks with the Sinclair company logo hauling drilling equipment into the Teapot Dome naval petroleum reserve. He asked U.S. Sen. John B. Kendrick, also a Democrat, to look into the matter. Kendrick, sensing wrongdoing, turned the question over to a special Senate investigating committee."[97]

President Harding avoided impeachment with a timely death. Albert Fall went to prison. The U.S Supreme Court eventually canceled the crooked leases though to do so it had to overturn the decision of a Wyoming federal court judge T. Blake Kennedy, a recent Harding appointee. Until Watergate, Teapot Dome was the scandal by which all others were compared. As it faded from mind, the Great Depression set in.

IT IS NOT THE FUNCTION OF THE GOVERNMENT TO
RELIEVE INDIVIDUALS OF THEIR RESPONSIBILITIES

The Depression actually hit Wyoming earlier than much of the nation. What, for some were "the Golden Twenties" or "the Roarin' Twenties," were, for others a time of economic hardship. In Wyoming, agricultural prices plummeted in 1920 causing hardships that were exacerbated by drought. When banks failed, there was no Federal Deposit Insurance Corporation (FDIC) to recover one's life savings. It would not come until 1933. By then dozens of Wyoming banks had been shuttered. Between 1920 and 1923, seventeen Wyoming banks failed, leaving depositors empty handed. Twenty-five more closed their doors in 1924 and by 1936, there were but 32 remaining banks of the 133 that did business in 1920. My parents lost the equity they had in a Salt Lake City home. The poverty in my family lasted a long time.

The 1920s saw the last hurrah for the coal-mining business as well. Wyoming historian, Dr. Phil Roberts, explains the times.

"Before 1910, every ship in the U. S. Navy fleet burned coal and then the government decided to switch to oil, ironically, with the monitor USS Wyoming (later USS Cheyenne). Jobs mining Wyoming coal peaked in 1922, at just over 9,100. Wyoming coal jobs dropped to almost nothing when the railroads completed transition from coal-fired steam locomotives to diesel in the early 1950s. Coal-mining jobs never returned to 1922 level."

All that was left of the storied Sweetwater coal mining history was the black lung disease that started to befall the miners who had spent those years breathing in the black dust.

According to Finnish humorist Tarja Moles, "Finns revel in hardship." If true, as the 1920s wore on, the Mottonens were in the right place. These second and third generation Finnish immigrants found themselves surrounded by government officials at the local and state levels who would rather their neighbors were suffering than to ask the federal government for help. To a great extent, 1935 Wyoming power brokers believed, as many of their heirs do today, what the immediate past President Herbert Hoover believed, that "it is not the function of the government to relieve individuals of their responsibilities."[98] It was a firm Wyoming philosophy, applied with no apparent sense of hypocrisy, to the needs of children and families but not to the building of railroads, raising of cattle, sheep, or crops, or mining all of which have always been deemed worthy of taxpayer subsidies.

THE MOST SERIOUS SITUATION IN ITS HISTORY

Hoover's philosophy, in the studied view of Wyoming historian T.A. Larson, "was accepted in Wyoming longer than elsewhere in the country."[99] Hoover's steadfast refusal to provide meaningful assistance to suffering families, a policy echoed by several Wyoming politicians, resulted in the President's defeat and Franklin Roosevelt's election in 1932. Just as the nation looked to a Democrat to save it from the continuing economic catastrophe, so did the voters of Wyoming. In the year FDR was elected to his first term, Democrat Leslie A. Miller was chosen to lead Wyoming. He was sworn-in in January 1933, and by December the new Governor figured out the state could no longer go it on its own.

An editorial in the December 8 *Wyoming Eagle* called the economic conditions confronting the state, "the most serious situation in its history." By then, we were all painfully aware that "thousands of cases of undernourished children" filled every community of the state. As a special session convened on December 4, 1933, to deal with the problems, Governor Miller told the Republican dominated legislature about those kids and the suffering of their families as he convened a special session to address the problems on December 4, 1933.

> *"There is abroad in our state a condition arising from long continued unemployment and the ravages of drouth more acute than generally realized, and I am*

convinced as of late that, as public servants, we have
failed to measure up to our responsibilities in these
matters."[100]

Wyoming had readily taken "millions of dollars as her share in farm aid."[101] Governor Miller chastised the GOP-led legislature for theirs being the only state having refused to accept funds from the Reconstruction Finance Corporation for relief projects "and in this fact we took considerable pride for some time" even though the state was experiencing "thousands of cases of undernourishment of children." The balance of the "Poor and Pauper Funds" in every county had been exhausted. The Democratic Governor asked the legislature for an appropriation of $75,000 to "provide food, clothing, fuel, and shelter to the needy and deserving in this period of great need." He proposed it be paid for with a four cent per gallon tax on beer. It would be the last time the legislature ever raised the beer tax but not the last time the legislature took pride in refusing federal funds to help low income citizens.

Unlike more conservative Wyoming counties, Sweetwater County welcomed both the Works Progress Administration (WPA) and the Civilian Conservation Corps (CCC), finding them to be "a great boon to the area."[102] The purpose of the WPA was to put people back to work doing jobs that benefited the entire community. WPA workers included not only laborers but, writers, musicians, and artists. The CCC was created to hire young, unemployed workers to undertake natural resource conservation projects. One of Lois's uncles worked in a CCC camp.

Wyoming journalist and historian Kerry Drake wrote about the contributions of the CCC. More than a thousand CCC workers built water and sewer projects, museums, phone lines and utility buildings, garbage pits and landfills, as well as recreation facilities, and wildlife conservation programs. They were always on call to risk their lives by fighting forest fires in the summer and rescuing stranded ranchers and travelers during winter blizzards.[103]

Despite these efforts, life in Depression-era Rock Springs was hard. My family was no exception, neither were we an exception to the fact that the people of the small mining community found creative ways to meet the challenge. In an essay called "Continuity and Change: The Great Depression," A. Dudley Gardner describes the response to the hardship of the Great Depression in Rock Springs, which found at least one in four Sweetwater County residents in need of public relief.

> *"In Rock Springs, people took collective action to provide people with homes. There is brief insight into a native son standing up to large and powerful monopolies who threatened free enterprise and thus the frontier spirit. Then there is the banker (John Hay) who did not foreclose on defaulted loans, maybe due to self-interest, but still Hay acted on his own perceptions of what was best for Rock Springs. Add to this the self-reliance of women who took it upon themselves to be providers and participants in an economic system that was in a state of crisis and a view of Wyoming's reaction to the difficulties faced in the 1930s emerges."*[104]

The Mottonens were aided by the self-reliant traits they inherited from their ancestors. My memories include few, if any of the hardships of the day. Life was quite simply what it was. People adjusted. Our family, like most of our neighbors, had no car and so the grocer came around once a week, knocking on doors and taking orders for delivery.

The day-to-day reports in the *Rock Springs Rocket* support my memory that life was fairly normal despite the economic upheaval. Stories spoke to the national debate FDR was having with Congress and the Supreme Court on his New Deal and occasionally about what the Wyoming legislature was doing or not doing about the crisis. But community life was more focused on normality. There were concerts featuring the Rock Springs symphony orchestra and dances, professional boxing matches, and other sporting events. Church life was active and civic organizations were thriving. Sadly, more than an occasional suicide occurred.

Crimes large and small made the front pages including everything from hitchhikers beating and robbing drivers to con-men scamming local businesses, burglaries and a thankfully rare murder. A mysterious man "with a slouched hat over his eyes" made us all nervous by following young girls home after school. The county clerk reported that "cupid wins by a big majority" as marriages outnumbered divorces by four to one. Sparsely settled areas of the county were beginning to get phone service. The Rialto movie theater had just installed new state of the art equipment showing "actors disporting themselves in action while talking direct to the audience." One of the first of the new age films was Al Jolson's "The Singing Fool."

The Union Pacific maintained a medical clinic in Rock Springs to serve miners and their families. UP also owned the grocery store, a pool hall, and a saloon, all of which charged the highest prices in town. Shopping at the company store meant my mother and the other wives paid more than a competitive price for groceries. Eggs sold for 25 cents a dozen, butter for 35 cents a pound, 12 large cans of milk cost a dollar, 2 pounds of hamburger sold for 45 cents, "Union Made" (as opposed to non-union made) bread was 45 cents for two jumbo loaves. Men's overalls could be purchased for a buck ten and work shirts for 89 cents. For those who couldn't afford a car, the Union Pacific "Overland Route" took families to Denver for a day at Elitch Gardens and Lakeside Park. For those who could afford a car, a Ford Roadster was priced $435, but a six-year-old Dodge Brothers Touring car set you back only $70. My parents found a used Model "A" Ford.

Even though women had served on Wyoming Territorial juries as early as 1870, a local state senator, Douglas A. Preston, made news when he led the charge to enact legislation depriving women of that right. Senator Preston, a lawyer, said he would personally welcome arguing a case before a jury that included women. "Yet at the same time, he knew jury room accommodations were not such as would very well permit women to serve on juries."[105] I suppose it was an early version of today's bathroom controversy.

Other local and state politicians were doing what they have always done; i.e. bashing the federal government. Following President Herbert Hoover's decision to limit oil and gas leases on some federal land, he went fishing and the local pols went howling. "Save Wyoming from Federal Invasion," pleaded one headline. Another said, "Autocratic Presidential Ruling on Oil Cancellation Provokes Most Doleful Wail Ever Heard in the West."[106] Although far more doleful wails have been heard since, those in 1929 were indeed loud.

ENDEAVORING

Not much of this changed the pursuit of happiness of first grader Lois Mottonen. When my family returned to Rock Springs from Winton, we moved into a house on Logan Avenue next door to my grandparents. Bitter Creek was nearby. It didn't have much water flowing except during summer rainstorms. Then the creek often overflowed its banks causing a great deal of damage to nearby homes and businesses. A March 29, 1936, letter I sent to Aunt Ellen, my mother's sister told the story of one such flood. "Boy did we get rain. We had a wash out. Grandfather's blacksmith shop was wash (sic) away."

I attended Roosevelt School, which was next to a large coal slag pile. A fire that burned in that pile there for many years pile was a huge local attraction. I have quite fond memories of very good teachers. Four women who taught at a time when teachers could be hired with only two years of college, combined to teach grades 1 through 5. I can still remember the charts on the walls of the classroom teaching kids how to write in cursive and how to make upper and lower-case letters, the small playground where the children played dodgeball, and the boys who threw snowballs at the girls. One day I retaliated, grabbing a handful of snow and a rock which I embedded in the ball of snow, squeezing it tightly into a large ball and heaving it at an offender. Blood flowed. I didn't do that again.

I'd come home with brown stains on my dress earned from sliding down the rusted playground slide. There were no school cafeterias in those days. Everyone went home for lunch. I have to say, I liked school from the very beginning, writing a letter to cousin Bobby, "I like school. I am in the first grade."

Using construction paper for the cover and pages of lined tablet, a class assignment required that I write a "paperback" book titled "Community Helpers." It was about the role of farmers, railroad engineers and motormen, postmen, "the healthman" or doctors, street sweepers, blacksmiths, butchers, and bakers. The work exhibited a youthful interest in life around us as well as an interest in doing research as I learned to express myself, traits that served me well in a career that lay ahead.

Soon, it was on to junior high. Fellow students formed an orchestra to play for school dances. The student body was a melting pot of all the various Rock Springs cultures. When I was 12 years old, I won a county spelling bee among 6th, 7th, and 8th graders. The next day I came down with the measles. The victory came with a $6 cash award, a photo in the *Rock Springs Daily Rocket*. It was the first $6 I ever earned. The school superintendent

Miners Homes along Bitter Creek
Photo courtesy of the American Heritage Center, University of Wyoming

drove me to Douglas to compete in the state contest. There, the word "endeavoring" proved my downfall. There were no organized after-school activities in those days. I took piano lessons from Lilian Wise. She had studied music at Oberlin after graduating from Rock Springs High School. Lillian was a member of a Sweetwater County pioneer family. She played background music during the silent movies at a local theater and at the dance hall as well as in the Rock Springs orchestra. I loved the piano and played during an occasional recital.

The measles left me with eyesight problems. Since there were no school nurses, the gym teacher used an eye chart to diagnose the need for my first pair of glasses. It was about this time I recall first hearing the dread word "cancer." School principal Isabell Hilling developed breast cancer.

The Mottonens were close-knit. Our family enjoyed holiday dinners at Grandma's. She baked bread and cinnamon rolls. My uncle had a boat which allowed us to catch fish regularly and camp around Half Moon and Fremont Lakes. Mother suffered from a hearing impairment brought about by a youthful case of strep throat. As a result, her social life was somewhat limited. She and neighbor women enjoyed coffee time together. Probably because of her hearing problem, she didn't like the movies as much as father who regularly went to the theater and brought me along.

My father worked hard during difficult times to care for his family. Before Winton, father attempted to supplement his income by starting a photography business. He was a good photographer with all the current state-of-the-art camera equipment but with most people having too little disposable income, the business never took off. Occasionally he clerked at a local store to make a few extra bucks. It was then he began reading books about carpentry and, over time, became skilled enough to work at the trade. In addition to his work in the mines, he drove the commuter bus transporting his fellow workers since few had access to a vehicle. My mother worked in two separate tailor shops where she made designer men's suits and cleaned clothes. Among the shop's customers were women who worked in the local brothels. I recall my mother "hated" cleaning their clothes.

My own work career started early as a clerk in a local drug store. One day a man came in and asked whether I had a union card. I became a member of the United Mine Workers of America as my father before me.

Young Lois with her mother Cecelia.

97 "The Teapot Dome Scandal' Phil Roberts, www.wyohistory.org/encyclopedia/teapot-dome-scandal; accessed December 8, 2016.

98 Larson, *History of Wyoming*, 443

99 Larson, *History of Wyoming*, 443

100 House Journal of the Special Session of the Twenty-second Legislature, Laramie Printing Co. (1933), 10-11

101 *Wyoming Eagle*, June 23, 1933, 12.

102 A. Dudley Gardner" Continuity and Change: The Great Depression, A brief Case Study of the New Deal and Wyoming Politics" www.wwcc.wy.edu/wyo_hist/depression3.htm, Accessed November 16, 2016.

103 Kerry Drake, *"Hard Times and Conservation: the CCC in Wyoming"* http://www.wyohistory.org/essays/hard-times-and-conservation-ccc-wyoming, accessed November 30, 2016.

104 Drake, *"Hard Times*

105 *Rock Springs Rocket*, February 13, 1929, 1 (all other references are to 1929 *Rock Springs Rocket* news stories).

106 *Rock Springs Rocket*, March 29, 1929, 1 and April 12, 1929, 1

CHAPTER SEVEN

IF ANY JAPS HAVE TO COME HERE WE WILL RUN
THEM THROUGH THE DIPPING VAT

No one who lived through it ever forgot where they were that day. It was a quiet Sunday afternoon in December at the Mottonen home. The radio played in the background, as it always did as the family sat down for lunch. We listened to static-filled sounds of the old second-hand radio that sat in the living room. Suddenly the whole world changed. At 12:22 PM Mountain Time this bulletin, itself interrupted so the operator could put through an emergency call, interrupted everyone's life.

Reporter: Hello, NBC. Hello, NBC. This is KTU in Honolulu, Hawaii. I am speaking from the roof of the Advertiser Publishing Company Building. We have witnessed this morning the distant view a brief full battle of Pearl Harbor and the severe bombing of Pearl Harbor by enemy planes, undoubtedly Japanese. The city of Honolulu has also been attacked and considerable damage done. This battle has been going on for nearly three hours. One of the bombs dropped within fifty feet of KTU tower. It is no joke. It is a real war. The public of Honolulu has been advised to keep in their homes and away from the Army and Navy. There has been serious fighting going on in the air and in the sea. The heavy shooting seems to be . . . a little interruption. We cannot estimate just how much damage has been done, but it has been a very severe attack. The Navy and Army appear now to have the air and the sea under control.

Operator: Ah, just a minute. This is the telephone company. This is the operator.

Reporter: *Yes.*

Operator: *We have quite a big call, an emergency call.*[107]

The Japanese had attacked the U.S. Navy Base in Hawaii. It was certainly a shock, but anyone reading the local newspaper could not have been too surprised. Leading up to December 7th, the front page of the *Rock Springs Daily Rocket* bugled a constant stream of reports about Nazi advances in Europe and toward Moscow, the sinking of U.S. ships in the Atlantic, and local men being drafted and sent away for training. Readers were aware of Japanese forces moving into the South Pacific as the Roosevelt Administration held talks with Japanese diplomats in Washington, D.C. They learned that those talks were collapsing on December 5th and that the Congress voted on the 6th to add two million more men to the U.S. Army the next day.

At the center of these negotiations was the father of a longtime Casper, Wyoming woman, advocate for peace on earth and women's rights. Mariko Miller was a young child when her father Hidenari Terasaki was the Japanese head of Western Intelligence and working in Washington, DC as the talks collapsed just as war was breaking out. Later, Mariko recounted how devastated her father was at the breakdown of peace talks and the invasion of Pearl Harbor. Soon after, the Terasaki family was back in Japan where they suffered great deprivation during World War II despite their social and political status. Mariko's parents removed her from grade school because it was the schoolhouse where the Japanese government found children to conscript for work in weapons manufacturing plants as the war continued.[108]

Writing a history of these times for Western Wyoming Community College, A. Dudley Gardner said,

> *"Unfortunately for the Japanese in the region, World War II brought with it increased racial tension. Possibly due to the diverse ethnic make-up of Rock*

Springs' population, the prejudice resulting from the Japanese bombing of Pearl Harbor, while evident, did not manifest itself in the extremes that marked other parts of the country."[109]

That may have been true but just down the road in the next county to the east and just a few months earlier, in June of 1940, a mob of more than a thousand men and boys in Rawlins attacked members of the Jehovah Witnesses because they were viewed as unpatriotic. One of the victims, called a "pioneer Rawlins businessman," was dragged from his home, forced to kiss an American flag and then severely beaten. Others were beaten and their property burned.[110] When they asked law enforcement officials for protection, they were put in a jail cell.

45 JAPS IN COUNTY REGISTER

Next the wrath was turned on Japanese-Americans. A Carbon County rancher made a dark suggestion, which was all too well received by Governor Nels Smith. "If any Japs have to come here we will run them through the dipping vat. We use an arsenic dip and for Japs we will step it up to a straight arsenic." Governor Smith replied. "It is most heartening to have the support of reasonable people on decisions of this character."[111]

Following the December 7th attack on Pearl Harbor, the tone of the reports in the *Rock Springs Daily Rocket* became immediately darker and more fearful. These were frightening times for a lot of people. Many folks in Sweetwater County were alarmed by reports that Japanese aircraft were spotted near California's coast. That same day, county sheriff. M.J. Dankowski was ordered by Governor Smith to require all Japanese aliens to immediately appear at the Sheriff's office to register themselves. A three-quarter page newspaper ad delivered the ominous message.

"Notice to all Alien Japanese. You are hereby required to appear at the Sheriff's Office in Rock Springs or

Green River for registration between the hours of 10 AM and 7:30 PM TODAY."

Furthermore, the Sheriff warned people of Japanese heritage living in the county that they were "prohibited from moving or attempting to move from your present locality." The Sheriff ordered bus and train companies not to sell tickets to Japanese passengers and to report any attempt any of them might make to book their way out of town. The message was as chilling as the 3-degree weather that enveloped the community that same day. The following day's headline announced, "45 Japs in County Register." A few days later, the Union Pacific ordered the local paymasters to freeze the pay of their Japanese miners. Before that month passed the railroad fired all of the Japanese workers and removed them from their UP provided homes. Because of the increasing demand for coal for the national defense efforts, Japanese employees were allowed to continue working the mines.[112]

The Veterans of Foreign Wars of Ogden, Utah, sent the recently elected Wyoming Governor Lester Hunt a resolution asking that, "all Japanese be placed in concentration camps and treated as prisoners of war."[113] The VFW in Rock Springs followed suit and assured the Governor that Wyoming veterans also endorsed the Utah resolution.[114]

It wasn't long before FDR ordered more than 120,000 Japanese Americans evacuated from the west coast. They had to go somewhere. Planning had started under Governor Smith who was clear. He didn't want them in his state. When Smith was informed of plans to relocate them to Wyoming, the Governor of the Equality State sent a telegram to Attorney General Francis Biddle, informing him in no uncertain terms that the state of Wyoming "cannot acquiesce to the importation of these Japanese into our state."[115]

Governor Smith learned what many Wyoming Governors have learned the hard way but yet refuse to acknowledge. They don't control federal policy. Smith's objections notwithstanding, Wyoming was one of the ten states selected to receive internees. The War Department acquired land between Cody and Powell in the far northwest corner of the state. It was called Heart Mountain. In his farewell speech on the day Hunt was inaugurated, Governor Smith took a parting shot, warning there would be "a serious social problem" if the Japanese-Americans were permitted to remain in Wyoming following the war. As Lester Hunt became Governor, the pot had been stirred, people were angry and positions were etched in stone.

Some wanted the Japanese-Americans to be treated as prisoners of war and placed under armed guard. Others wanted to use them for farm labor and to build highways. Some merchants wanted them to spend money in their stores. Others wanted them banned from entering their nearby towns. In May of 1943, the town councils of Powell and Cody petitioned Hunt to halt the issuance of passes allowing internees to visit their communities.[116] Initially, Hunt asked camp director Guy Robertson to restrict "permission allowing evacuees to visit Powell and Cody." Robertson politely explained, "There are two sides to the question." Robertson found quickly that there were business people who wanted the dollars the Japanese had to spend and farmers who wanted them to work their farms. Others didn't want to see the Japanese in their community for any reason whatsoever.

The Governor began to hear from those who disagreed with their town councils. "As you no doubt are aware of the Anti-Heart Mountain War Relocation Camp Mayor we have," wrote A.R. Fryer of Fryer's Pharmacy in Powell, "there happen to be a few other details which I think should be brought to your attention at this time since our Honorable Mayor and City Council are again trying to kick up more trouble concerning said Camp and its citizens." Fryer informed the Governor the camp had provided an economic boom to the businesses of Park County, explaining "90% of the merchants here in Powell have been able to pay off their old debts and now buy War Bonds since this Relocation camp was built two years ago." To make himself clear this was an economic and not a social justice issue, Fryer assured Hunt the business community favored the evacuees over "these Mexican Nationals brought up from Mexico that can't even talk United States (sic), then steal you blind the minute they come into your store."[117]

Other merchants agreed. They appreciated the extra income received from the internees and hastened to assure the Governor their town council did not speak for the majority. Nevertheless, the mayor continued to insist the evacuees be banned from visiting Powell. In August 1944, Hunt decided to commission a private investigator to determine which side was right. Hunt made this promise to the mayor. "If his report substantiates your position, I will immediately follow your suggestions with reference to asking the Heart Mountain authorities to discontinue allowing the Japanese to visit Powell." The mayor felt certain that if the inquiries were "thorough and unbiased" his position would prevail. He agreed with Hunt's strategy.

Captain William Bradley of the Wyoming Highway Patrol was dispatched to Powell. He interviewed "perhaps twenty people" chosen at random and allowed to remain anonymous. Many didn't care one way or another, Bradley reported to the Governor. Others told him, "Every Jap should be taken out and shot." Many others had no objection. Bradley reported, "I was given the impression that the larger majority of the townspeople were in favor of having the Japs come to Powell to trade." He estimated the split to be about 65% to 35% opposed to the Mayor's position.

Hunt told the mayor he was now "more stymied than ever on what I should do." He promised to take "drastic action to see that the Japs leave the relocation Center and Wyoming immediately after the termination of the war." In the meantime, the Governor bowed out of the community controversy. Regardless, the presence of so many Japanese-Americans in Park County continued to stir controversy. The Governor received countless petitions and letters demanding he assure them all the evacuees would be required to leave Wyoming at war's end.

Of course, the Governor had no such authority. The question of whether any of the evacuees would be allowed to remain in Wyoming had long been an issue. During the gubernatorial campaign of 1942, Governor Smith told a Cody audience he had received written assurance from the U.S. Government that all internees would be required to leave Wyoming at the end of the war. No such document was ever located. No such legal authority existed. Governors Smith and Hunt each refused to acknowledge that after the war, as American citizens, the evacuees were free to live anywhere in the country they might choose. Some, not many, chose Wyoming.

In July 1945, with the war nearly over, the Powell chapter of American War Dads petitioned the Governor to "not impose these people on the Fathers and Mothers of this community now at a time when many of them are being advised of the death of their sons and daughters in our war against Japan." Governor Hunt forwarded the petition to Guy Robertson asking what "the process or method is in returning the Japs."

Mr. Robertson assured the Governor the camp would be closed on or before November 15. But he had run out of patience with the Park County complainers. Robertson reminded the Governor the men and women at issue were U.S. citizens who had been forced from their homes. He recounted how many of their sons were still fighting and dying in the South Pacific. "758 boys from families in Heart Mountain are now fighting in our armed forces all over the world, and I venture to suggest that these boys are just as dear to their War dads and mothers as are the boys from Powell or any other community to theirs."

Mr. Robertson asked, "if some fanatical, race baiting, unthinking and unprincipled individual did not instigate the petition and by canvassing the highways and byways of Powell and by cajolery and false information prevail upon these people to sign something that sober reflection and study might cause them to hang their heads in embarrassment and shame."

The last train, filled with more than 400 Japanese-Americans, left Heart Mountain for the west coast on November 9, 1945. A handful chose to remain in Wyoming where they became contributing citizens but all the former residents of Heart Mountain had been relocated. The water was turned off, the boilers drained, the windows of the barracks boarded up and the mess hall closed. One of the sorriest chapters in Wyoming and U.S. history came to an end.

I feel even greater sadness about this entire episode today. I understood that shortly after Pearl Harbor both Democratic and Republican politicians thought the Japanese were a threat to this country. However, I never understood how a free people, could stand by either quietly acquiescing or full participating in the injustice could permit our government to confiscate the homes and businesses of Japanese-Americans as they were forced to board a train with but one suitcase of their belongings and move form from California to Heart Mountain in Wyoming. There the government forced them to live in a one-room clapboard house covered with tar paper. Winters there were very cold and they did not have appropriate winter clothing.

But, in all honesty, violations of civil rights are still prevalent in this country. Only the target changes. Today it's Muslims and undocumented families as well as refugees. Tomorrow it will be someone else.

It was a sorry chapter in U.S. and Wyoming history leaving both with a black eye. Although Congress formally apologized and paid compensation to the former internees, Heart Mountain remains a lesson unlearned.

Not surprisingly, war news occupied the papers as it occupied everyone's thoughts and conversations. The federal Office of Civilian Defense busied itself educating people in Rock Springs and elsewhere on what they should do in the event there was an air raid over the county. We all watched in tears as Sweetwater County people marched off to war. The newspaper touted everyone who enlisted or was drafted. The wave of patriotism was so strong that state education officials felt the need to encourage youngsters to complete their studies before enlisting. "This additional training will make it possible for them to enter a more highly specialized field of service when they answer their country's call."

One of our Rock Springs' neighbors, Russell Vaughn Cornford was reported to be the first Sweetwater County resident "dead or missing."[118] A few days later, the War Department corrected itself. Russell Vaughn Cornford's parents were overjoyed to hear their son was among the living. However, Louis Besso's parents, in turn, got the bad news. Their son was the first.

The Selective Service Act authorizing the draft for military service was enacted in September of 1940 and renewed a few months before Pearl Harbor by a single vote margin in the U.S. House of Representatives. Two of my uncles, and an aunt, along with some cousins quickly joined millions of Americans lining up to enlist in the armed services. Another uncle was turned down for medical reasons. With the war, the nation's demand for coal soared. My father, then 38 years-old and at the upper limit in the age restriction imposed by the Selective Service Act, remained in Sweetwater County to do his part to meet that demand. So did others. Likely because of its coal mining jobs, Sweetwater County was one of the few Wyoming counties that didn't lose population during the war years.

Everyone tried to go on with life as the dark clouds of the war hung over them. By now a junior high student, I went off to school every morning. Dad went off to work. Mom tended house. Folks went to church and concerts, high school basketball games, and movies. To my knowledge, Japanese-American classmates were not marginalized in our community, though looking back on it, I suspect many suffered quietly. Winton miners raised $15,000 for the purchase of War Bonds. Dad and his fellow miners held a meeting of the United Mine Workers and voted to give a day's pay or about $2000 to President Roosevelt for "the national defense."[119] The Boy Scouts and others helped in bond drives and many Sweetwater residents grew Victory Gardens, rationed gasoline and nylons, and prayed for the men and women in harm's way. And so it went through the toughest years of the War.

D-Day, June 6, 1944 was a Tuesday. The people of Southwestern Wyoming, it was reported the next day in the Rock

Springs newspaper, received their first notice of the invasion "early Tuesday morning when they picked up the *Daily Rocket* from their front porches." I recall how abruptly the mood of the community changed. Newspaper ads asked for prayers for the men on Normandy beach and the other beaches where Allied troops were fighting. "The invasion is on," said one pitching for the purchase of War Bonds. "Give 'em what you've got." A graphic picture depicted an American G.I. driving a bayonet into the heart of a German soldier. "Drive it home," the ad said. Each day the news was a cause for increased optimism. The war might end soon.

Then came the death of President Roosevelt, followed quickly by the Nazi surrender. The war in Europe was over. Many Sweetwater County soldiers would soon be home, but not those fighting in the Pacific. That war continued until President Harry Truman ordered that atomic bombs be used to persuade the Japanese government to throw in the towel.

107 "This Is No Joke: This Is War": A Live Radio Broadcast of the Attack on Pearl Harbor, http://historymatters.gmu.edu/d/5167, accessed January 12, 2017.

108 Kathleen Kelleher, "Found in Translation: History: A Japanese diplomat's writings about Emperor Hirohito fill in some blanks in World War II records," *Los Angeles Times,* March 21, 1991,
http://articles.latimes.com/1991-03-21/news/vw-794_1_world-war-ii-records, accessed June 2, 2017.

109 A. Dudley Gardner, *"The Japanese in Southwestern Wyoming"* Western Wyoming Community College, http://www.wwcc.wy.edu/wyo_hist/japanese4.htm

110 "Members of Religious Sect Made to Kiss Flag in Wyoming" *Corpus Christi Times,* June 19, 1940, 1.

111 Letter from William D. Sidley of the Silver Spur Ranch, Encampment, Wyoming, dated March 14, 1942, and Letter from Governor Smith to William D. Sidley, dated March 30, 1942, Box 3, Papers of Nels Smith, American Heritage Center, University of Wyoming.

112 Gardner, *"The Japanese in Southwestern Wyoming"*

113 "Resolution" dated September 1, 1943 Sent to Hunt by Corporal Fred J. Grant Post 1481, Veterans of Foreign Wars, Ogden, Utah, File: "Heart Mountain" Box 1, Lester C. Hunt Papers, American Heritage Center, University of Wyoming.

114 Letter to Hunt from F.H. Dennison, Adjutant, VFW Post 2316, Rock Springs, Wyoming, dated November 30, 1943, Box 1, Hunt Papers, AHC.

115 Telegram from Smith to Francis Biddle, Attorney General of the United States, February 21, 1942, Box 3, Papers of Nels Smith, American Heritage Center, University of Wyoming.

116 "Resolution of Policy Toward Japanese at Heart Mountain Relocation Center" File: "Heart Mountain" Box 1, Hunt Papers, AHC.

117 Letter from A.R. Fryer to Governor Hunt, June 21, 1944, Box 1, Hunt papers, AHC.

118 T.A. Larson, *Wyoming's War Years 1941-1945*, Wyoming Historical Foundation (1993), 9

119 Larson, *Wyoming's War Years*, 11

CHAPTER EIGHT

A GIRL IS SHE, WITH QUIET WAYS

As the people of Rock Springs joined the rest of the world celebrating the end of World War II, my classmates and I finished our junior year at Rock Springs High School and headed into an exciting senior year. The times were so different that today's high school students and their parents would not recognize them. A community of immigrants, Rock Springs evidenced a strong valuing of education. Parents didn't want their children to follow them into mining or railroad jobs. They made certain their children adhered to high standards of discipline. We never witnessed a fist fight on school grounds. Children were expected to behave in school, and most did.

Neither of my parents had completed high school but they expected not only that I would graduate but that I would do well enough to go on to college. Father also thought it important that his daughter take classes that would help her get a job later. Thus, I enrolled in a shorthand and typing as well as bookkeeping classes. Father had but two ironclad rules. His daughter could neither smoke cigarettes nor get married. I never did either.

I enjoyed school, studied hard, and challenged myself. All report cards, from Kindergarten through the 12th grade, reflect an "A" student with nothing less than an occasional "B" and seldom more than one or two absences in a school year. Teachers frequently praised my citizenship and helpful attitude. Fearing I was overly shy, I signed up for a theater class, playing the statue of the Virgin Mary in a 1946 Christmas pageant at the school. Schools in those days didn't provide lunches. Kids walked home for lunch. There were no school buses serving any part of town and so all students walked to school every day regardless of the distance or the weather.

The Mottonen home was more than a mile from the school on McCarty Street. It was a four-room house sitting on a lot purchased for $65 and built with a loan of $2500. Mother hung clothes on a rope line in the backyard as neighbors set fire to their trash in the alley causing the laundry to smell bad. One neighbor had a wine-press where carloads of grapes were brought to be turned into wine for the annual community wine festival.

CLEAN UP ALL ALLEYS, REMOVE ALL GARBAGE, GET RID OF MANURE PILES, AND SPRAY WITH DDT

Not all was idyllic. Polio struck our family as it struck many thousands of families across America. One of my uncles returned safely from combat in the Pacific only to learn he had the frightening disease. We all witnessed friends dying, others wearing the heavy metal braces used to stabilize victims of the frightful disease. It was made even scarier because no one understood its source. Even the medical researchers and physicians were guessing about both cause and treatment. Dr. Jonas Salk hadn't yet begun his research which would answer those questions. That was a few years away when Wyoming's top health officer, Dr. G.M. Anderson issued a warning to worried people like the Mottonens. "It behooves every Wyoming community," he advised, "to take extraordinary efforts to clean up all alleys, remove all garbage, get rid of manure piles, and spray with DDT barns, cafes, milk stations, and all other places where food is handled."[120]

While public health workers were spraying the town with DDT, I was working in a hospital office around the corner from the polio ward, which was not isolated from exposure. Some 15 years after thousands of food handling sites were sprayed with DDT in an ineffective and dishearteningly harmful way to stop polio, Rachel Carson published her book *Silent Spring*. Carson documented DDT as a cause of cancer. Its use wasn't banned until 1992. Dr. Salk's polio vaccine was introduced in 1952.

Many of the parents of fellow students were first, or like mine, second generation immigrants. Their children are pictured in my yearbooks with names like Mrak, Mazankis, Goich, Bertagnolli,

Botero, Okano, and Mottonen along with a Thomas, McFadden and a Henderson. The cultural diversity we experienced at a young age formed much of a worldview that would serve us well throughout our lives. Nonetheless, it was at Rock Springs High School that I first felt the sting of discrimination. I served on the student council, called "the Student Board of Control," and was the student body treasurer while excelling in my studies. Even so, a teacher who didn't think that was a place for girls, denied my request for enrollment in a physics class. I objected heartily and he relented.

When, at long last, high school graduation arrived, ceremonies followed a week of dinners and parties feting the grads. The *Daily Rocket* reported, "The week before graduation has finally arrived for seniors in Rock Springs. Mothers began to breathe a sigh of relief and fathers reluctantly yield to the costs."

At the end of a long week of celebrations, Rock Springs High held its annual award's ceremony. I was given a special medal by classmates. The last day of high school rolled around on May 29, 1947. One hundred forty-four students, including 23 World War II veterans, donned caps and gowns, walking down the aisle to a medley of classic Southern songs. I was one of six students given University of Wyoming scholarships that day. My senior year school yearbook, the 1947 *Sagebrusher,* described me with a poem.

> *"A girl is she, with quiet ways.*
> *Her motto is 'silence pays.'*
> *When others chat throughout the day*
> *She listens and gets A's"*

The summer passed quickly as I worked full time at the Rock Springs hospital. Soon I was hauling a trunk loaded with clothing and personal treasures, and was off for Laramie where, after the long train ride from Rock Springs, I walked through the doors of Old Main to enroll at the University of Wyoming.

HAUNTED BY THE EXPANDING FUTURE AND
MALTREATED BY THE SHIFTING PRESENT

Old Main opened on September 6, 1887. When I arrived for that freshman year in the fall of 1947, the four-story building was much the same as it was when the first UW students walked through the doors six decades ago although it was undergoing a major renovation. A new president had been installed at UW a couple of years earlier. George Duke Humphrey gave his first address to the University community the day World War II ended. He would earn his place in history as one of the school's giants.

But for the United States Supreme Court, I might have gone to the University of Wyoming, not in Laramie, but in Lander. Someone in that picturesque central Wyoming community did his or her homework and found reference to an 1892 congressional vote earmarking federal funds to what was called the "Agricultural College of Wyoming." Lander had been the home of Lander Agricultural College at the time. It seemed to hopeful people in Lander that Congress intended that school be the University and so a few of them filed a lawsuit seeking to move the University from Laramie. Eventually the U.S. Supreme Court told the citizens of Lander that the law didn't mean what it said, that the appropriation was actually intended to belong to the state and not to their "Agricultural College of Wyoming." Since the state had decided to allocate the dollars to the University at Laramie, it would be Wyoming's only four-year college.[121]

So, it was off to Laramie, not Lander.

As with most colleges and universities in those days, the war's end gave birth to extraordinarily large student enrollment at the University of Wyoming. Enrollment tripled, as did the challenges of meeting the immediate needs of so many students. UW's 1946 Yearbook cleverly described the faculty and deans as "haunted by the expanding future and maltreated by the shifting present." Dr. Humphrey told the community that among the new enrollees, there were two types of students. He said there "is a group of older, more serious students who will demand a more efficient type of instruction." The second group was comprised of "recently-graduated high school students who might find the pace of the veterans too fast for them."

The campus was overflowing with young men, fresh from the war, eager to resume their lives, restarting them on the campus. They had GI money to pay for their tuition but needed housing and jobs. The University President pleaded for community employers to offer the students part time jobs as he quickly hired a large number of new faculty members while searching for classrooms and housing to accommodate the new enrollees.

Housing students was as big a challenge as teaching them. The *Laramie Republican and Boomerang* ran front page appeals for local folks to rent rooms to incoming students.

> *"Without the cooperation of Laramie households, hundreds of Wyoming young people will be denied the privilege of attending the University this fall."*

The newspaper reminded residents that each student who came to town meant an annual economic benefit to the community equal to one-thousand dollars.

The Laramie Chamber of Commerce donated fifty trailer houses, adding capacity to the new dormitories built expeditiously by the school. "Even a water tower behind Dray's Cottage where Washakie Center is now located was remodeled and occupied."[122] Although locals complained about how unattractive they were, butler huts were thrown up between the Student Union and Ivinson Avenue to provide housing specifically reserved for returning veterans. Classrooms and labs were being built as fast as humanly possible.

In those early postwar days, the University of Wyoming attracted significant scholars to its faculty. A woman who had recently received a Ph.D. from the University of Chicago headed the history department. Dr. Laura White was 26 years old when, in 1924, she became the head of a one-person department that grew over the years. She hired a second member for the department in 1925. Frederick L. Nussbaum earned a graduate degree at the University of Pennsylvania and taught at Northwestern, Temple, and the University of Southern California before coming to Laramie. Nussbaum wrote a book on the French Revolution, which won the prestigious Henry Baxter Adams Award. He was on sabbatical when Dr. T.A. Larson was hired.[123]

Larson became the preeminent Wyoming historian and a state legislator. A young teacher from Nebraska named Gale McGee came to teach history. In 1958, McGee became one of Wyoming's two United States Senators and served for 18 years.

THE LITTLE RED SCHOOL HOUSE
IS REDDER THAN YOU THINK

I'd been a freshman only a couple of months, when in early October of 1947, a then little-known Wisconsin Senator named Joe McCarthy had an impact on Wyoming. The National Association of University Governing Boards sponsored a conference at the University of Michigan that month. It was nearly three years ahead of Senator McCarthy's Wheeling, West Virginia speech when the Republican demagogue claimed to have a list of known Communists employed by the U.S. State Department. McCarthy wasn't the one who started American worries about Communists and their potential influence in our country. Ahead of McCarthy, President Harry Truman issued an Executive Order requiring loyalty reviews of federal employees. The national hysteria about Communism was percolating even in little Laramie, Wyoming.

One of the speakers at the Michigan conference gave an address he titled provocatively "The Little Red Schoolhouse Is Redder Than You Think." UW's board of trustee's president Milward Simpson and trustee Harold Del Monte were in the audience that day. The speaker issued a warning. It seemed subversive books were lining the shelves of the libraries of the schools for which the audience of college trustees had responsibility.

Simpson and Del Monte arrived back in Laramie with a great deal of angst about what they'd heard. The topic was placed on the agenda for the next board meeting. On October 25, 1947, the trustees gathered in the boardroom of Old Main. Simpson called the meeting to order. "Dr. (P.M.) Cunningham moved that President Humphrey appoint a committee to read and examine textbooks in use at the University of Wyoming, in the field of social sciences, to determine if such books are subversive or un-American. The motion was seconded by Mr. Del Monte and carried."[124] The meeting adjourned. Shortly thereafter, all hell broke loose.

Almost immediately there was a tidal wave of negative attention. Criticism came from far and near. Newspapers in at least twenty communities around the U.S. harshly criticized the University.[125] The criticism was even greater at home.

UW President Humphrey implemented the board's resolution. A panel headed by UW Law School Dean Robert promptly demanded department heads develop a list of required texts. The school's leaders had stepped into a mess they had not anticipated. The board members saved face by appointing a group of professors to review some books and report back. They read 64 books, provided the board with their assurance they contained no anti-American or subversive information and the matter was laid to rest.

"That's fine," said McCracken. "Now the people of Wyoming will know that even though subversive teaching may be practiced at other schools, there is none of it in Wyoming."[126] It was over. But the pain visited on Wyoming by Joe McCarthy wouldn't end there. Many in Wyoming continued worrying about the Reds until Donald Trump told them it wasn't necessary any longer.

I RECALL THE SHOCK WHEN I WENT TO COLLEGE AND DISCOVERED HOW SOPHISTICATED THE CHEYENNE STUDENTS WERE

Life in the University environment was more than a little stimulating. It immediately became apparent that students from

Wyoming's larger communities like Casper and Cheyenne were better prepared for college than those of us from smaller towns like Rock Springs. One of those students was Walter C. Urbigkit, who went on to become an esteemed state legislator and a Justice on the Wyoming Supreme Court. For my part, the realization came hard. I was a naive kid who grew up in a town with few amenities. I recall the shock when I went to college and discovered how sophisticated the Cheyenne students were. Even so, the study habits I learned back home served me well and the gap was quickly bridged.

Laramie opened exciting cultural doors for me. I had always been a curious young woman. So, Laramie was a delight. There were three movie theaters. Between the Crown, Fox, and Varsity screens, this young woman who grew to love movies, going to theaters with her father could see the latest Hollywood films featuring the biggest movie stars of the day. On those three large screens, I saw Bing Crosby, Bob Hope, Gary Cooper, Barbara Stanwyck, Dorothy Lamour among others.

At the UW liberal arts auditorium, we saw Laurence Olivier in "Henry IV." Spike Jones and his "Musical Depreciation Revue" played a live concert at the University. Especially enjoyable were the weekly dances at the Elks and Eagles Clubs. Dr. Gale McGee lectured the Soroptimist Club's Founders Week celebration with his fine oratorical skill. The title of his speech was "Pearl Harbor Revisited." Laramie also had a darker side of which we were made aware. The town didn't outlaw prostitution until the mid-1950s, so we noticed there were also plenty of brothels.[127]

The patriotic community supported President Truman's 1947 call to help feed starving post-war Europeans by eating less in the United States and sending the surplus to Europe. The President asked Americans to follow a four-step strategy. If we went to a restaurant on a Tuesday, for example, most served no meat. You couldn't order poultry or eggs on Thursdays. Bread and butter were provided only "on request." We were urged to save a slice of bread every day. Most of Laramie's restaurants agreed and refused to serve meat, poultry, or eggs on the designated days.

As it is now, Laramie was then filled with sports fanatics. Indicative was the way in which nearly every business closed for the local high school's homecoming parade. Because the University of Wyoming was then, as now, the only four-year university in the state, it was the school's football team that drew the most fan interest. The team we now refer to as the Pokes, was then called "the Punchers," an apparent reference to "cow punchers." They wore uniforms of gold colored shirts with silver pants. Unlike today, the team was largely home grown. All but 15 of the 42-man roster came from Wyoming high schools. They were coached by the legendary Bowden Wyatt. My first year at UW was also Wyatt's first season with the Punchers. He started his UW career with two straight 4-5 seasons before taking an undefeated team to a victory in the 1950 Gator Bowl in my senior year.

At the time, the biggest project on campus was the drive started in 1947 to build "a living memorial to the men and women who served in World War II." Governor Lester Hunt, Coach Wyatt, and UW's athletic director Red Jacoby combined forces to raise the money to build both the Fieldhouse and War Memorial Stadium.

Being involved in activities was always important to me. They provided opportunities to meet new people, make new friends, and to learn new things. I found a home at the Chi Omega Sorority, the largest sorority in the United States, which calls itself "an international women's organization forever committed to our founding purposes." They were friendship, personal integrity, service to others, and academic excellence and intellectual pursuit. Chi Omega gave me a place to live and meals to eat for $60 per month, a barely affordable amount. As in high school, I quickly became a leader, described in the 1951 UW yearbook as one of "the most prominent Chi O's." I was elected sorority president in my senior year. I gave the credit to my parents in a March 1, 1950 letter informing them of my election. "You my parents, can never know how very much you have given me by giving me the opportunity for a college education." They had not had that opportunity themselves and I never failed to acknowledge the sacrifices they made so that I could get a good education.

I was also a member of Phi Gamma Nu. The 1951 Wyoming year book described the organization as "For women only—the brainy ones." Members planned careers in business and commerce. Likewise, I was also an active member of the campus organization promoting involvement in intramural sports.

Few, if any, students had cars. Everyone walked everywhere. I studied accounting, tax, and contract law. Especially enjoyable was a class in poetry. The professor eventually wrote a poem about each of the students. Not unlike the poem in my high school yearbook, the theme of this one was what was perceived as my mysterious nature, which was actually shyness.

For a while I dated a law student from Fremont County. We spent a great deal of time together, dancing and at other social events. He worked, as I recall, at a downtown shoe store, near where the brothels were located. Among his clients were some of Laramie's "ladies of the night," who were quite fashion conscious. He was always happy to see them, if only because he worked on a commission. He also made a few dollars driving cars from a Rapid City dealership to new owners in Laramie. Whenever his parents came to Laramie, the four of us had dinner together. Then one day in the summer after graduation, out of the blue, there came a "Dear Jane" letter. With little explanation, the relationship ended as suddenly as it began.

THERE WAS NO END IN SIGHT

Perhaps the most memorable time of my college days' experiences was the Blizzard of '49. On New Year's Day, it snowed about four inches in Laramie and the winds whipped up a normal winter white out. Roads were closed though that alone was not a particularly uncommon thing this time of the year. We didn't think much about it. The weather forecast was reassuring. The storm, it said would end that evening. They were wrong. It didn't end for nearly two months.

I rode into the eye of the storm seated comfortably in a passenger train returning to Laramie after Christmas break with family in Rock Springs on January 2. As the train made its way east from Rock Springs, the clouds darkened. The snow fall became more and more intense. You could see this was something different from the usual December snow. It was near the end of the first day of the historic storm, that the train limped into the depot at Laramie. As we disembarked, I noticed there were no taxi cabs awaiting passengers as was normal. I joined others trudging the two miles to the sorority house dragging a heavy suitcase through the deepening snow and howling winds. I realized we had been fortunate that the train made it to Laramie. By then most roads in and out of Laramie and across Wyoming were closed by 60 miles per hour gusts and blinding snow and every other scheduled train found it impossible to move through the huge snow drifts.

By the next day, the blizzard shut down Laramie and much of Wyoming as well as many of the surrounding states. New storms followed and the weather bureau warned "there was no end in sight." The streets around us were empty of everything but the large, imposing snow drifts. Traffic came to a halt and we had to eat whatever remained in the storage cupboard. I assure you that none of those menus ever made it into a gourmet cookbook. We worried about the returning veterans who were still housed in Quonset huts with little or no insulation. What was for us an inconvenience, was much more than that for those veterans and so many others.

By the end of the first week, nine Wyomingites were dead because of the harsh weather and relentless cold. Before it ended, a dozen people lost their lives in the state. The misery index rose day after day as trucks, cars, and passenger trains were stranded throughout Laramie and the state. The good Laramie citizens rallied to feed them and opened the doors of their own homes to travelers as the hotels and motels filled to overflow.

Each day it seemed to worsen. Each day more snow fell and temperatures continued to plummet. The blizzard was the front-page news everyone in Laramie read each morning. The *Laramie Republican and Boomerang's* reporters spent long hours investigating stories about hardships falling on humans and animals, livestock as well as wildlife. The National Guard and the Fifth U.S. Army came to help clear roads and rescue victims. It was not until late February, some two months after it started, that the storm was, at long last, not the most prominent news.[128]

While all university classes were canceled initially, the University eventually re-opened and students marched through high snow drifts to classrooms. Life slowly returned to normal. Meanwhile back in Sweetwater County, there was another development reminding those who were interested that it had been some time since the Equality State acted like it deserved the motto.

Blizzard of '49
Photo courtesy of the American Heritage Center, University of Wyoming

…IF IT WOULDN'T HAVE BEEN FOR
THOSE DAMN WOMEN

To this very day, some Wyoming people take great pride in recalling that the state was the first to allow women to serve on a jury. It was 1870. Wyoming was a territory. It was a Grand Jury, a legal body empaneled to determine whether criminal charges should be filed against a citizen. A woman was seated on the panel only after she overcame a motion to prohibit "integration of the jury." The Chief Justice denied the motion reasoning, "It seems to be eminently proper for women to sit on Grand Juries, which will give them the best possible opportunity to aid in suppressing the dens of infamy which curse the county."[129] It would be 80 years before another Wyoming woman would be given another "opportunity to aid in suppressing the dens of infamy which curse the county" by serving on a jury of any kind.

That woman was from my home county. It was May of 1950. Louise Spinner Graf was not happy when she received the summons to appear for possible jury duty. The trial started on a Monday and that was her wash day. The Sheriff who delivered the summons assured her that was not a good reason to ignore the summons. So, on Monday morning, Mrs. Graf arrived at the Sweetwater County courthouse. She spoke about the experience to Wyoming historian Bill Barton 25 years later.

"[I]t seemed that there were two fellows coming from Rock Springs and they had been drinking, and they stopped halfway between here and Rock Springs and got out of the car. And one shot the other, and killed him, and that was it. And so, it went on. It lasted for about two days. And when we went into the room in the back, they—one of the men from Farson, [Wyo.]— you know since this is the first woman—first jury with women—I think there were five women and seven men—well, eight would be all, wouldn't it? And they said that we should have a woman foreman. And one

*other one spoke up and said that they thought that
I should be—because having lived here so long, and
my people having been here so long. And I said oh no.
You know, I had never even been to a jury. I had never
even been in a courtroom. I didn't even know what a
courtroom was like, let alone a jury. And I said oh my
gosh, I wouldn't know what to do. And they said oh
we'll help you, you'll get along all right. All right, it
went on and of course we found him guilty. And the
judge gave him the sentence.*[130]

Mrs. Graf told Barton that the defense lawyer, who had never
before lost a murder case, blamed it on the women on the jury,
saying "he would never have lost that murder case if it wouldn't
have been for those damn women."

"Those damn women" was the sort of attitude many women
confronted as we entered the job market. The fact that I carried
with me an accounting degree won with honors from the University
of Wyoming didn't seem to matter in 1951.

---

120 "Wyoming Health Director Urges Polio Clean-up," *Rock Springs Daily Rocket,* May 16, 2947, 13.

121 "110 Years Ago: United States Supreme Court Keeps The University of Wyoming in Laramie," http://laramielive.com/110-years-ago-united-states-supreme-court-keeps-the-university-of-wyoming-in-laramie/?trackback=fbshare_mobile_top&trackback=tsmclip, accessed June 1, 2017.

122 Deborah Hardy, *Wyoming University: The First 100 Years 1886-1986* (University of Wyoming 1986), 146.

123 *Commercial Policy in the French Revolution* was among many books written by Nussbaum. The copyright page of a current edition published by BiblioBazaar in September 24, 2009, says, "We believe this work is culturally important and have elected to bring the book back into print as part of our continuing commitment to the preservation of printed works worldwide." http://www.amazon.com/Commercial-Policy-French-Revolution-Career/dp/1113661976/ref=sr_1_1?s=books&ie=UTF8&qid=1421245164&sr=1-1 accessed on January 14, 2015.

124 The University of Wyoming Minutes of the Trustees, October 24-25, 1947, http://www.uwyo.edu/trustees/board-meeting-archives/1940-1949-minutes/1947-board-of-trustees-meetings.html, accessed January 13, 2015.

125 *Common Sense,* January 19, 1948, *Common Sense* was a short-lived publication by

University of Wyoming students. Its purpose was to oppose the book investigation. The student publisher was Walter G. Urbigkit who later became a state legislator and a Justice on the Wyoming Supreme Court.

126 "UW Faculty Committee Maintains Book Probe Hearing Still Needed" *The Laramie Republican Boomerang*, January 21, 1948, 1.

127 "Women of the West-Preserving Western History," Edited by Andrew Gulliford, University of New Mexico Press (2005), 197

128 Much of the information in this section comes from the *Laramie Republican and Boomerang* issues in January and February 1949.

129 "Timeline of Legal History of Women in the United States" http://www.iasb. uscourts.gov/v2_community/WHMsection5.4.pdf, Accessed February 17, 2017.

130 Bill Barton, "Louise Graf, Jury Forman and Green River Citizen" http://www. wyohistory.org/oral-histories/louise-graf-jury-foreman-and-green-river-citizen, Accessed February 17, 2017.

CHAPTER NINE

WOMEN NEED NOT APPLY

After graduating from the University of Wyoming, I came to Cheyenne with two suitcases and a trunk, but no car or place to live. I spent my first two nights sleeping at the home of a friend who had an apartment in the residential section near the hospital.

Cheyenne was by far the biggest city I had ever lived in. Cheyenne at just a few folks short of 32 thousand people was twice the size of Laramie and three times the size of Rock Springs. The Cheyenne newspaper warned of a possible polio epidemic. Sloan's Lake at Lion's Park, a popular swimming hole, closed for fear of the dreaded disease. Cheyenne judges were concerned mostly about drunk drivers, illegal gambling, and double parking.

That summer was my first Cheyenne Frontier Days. Seems I came at the right time. The Wyoming Tribune said that "even hardened Cheyenne natives, accustomed to a week of spectacular shenanigans, have climbed aboard this year's star-studded rodeo wagon."

Movie star Fred MacMurry, the star of the wholesome television series, "My Three Sons," came to town to crown Miss Frontier, Laura Bailey, and Jane Henderson, her "Lady in Waiting." They said more than 10,000 people lined the streets to see him. Lawrence Welk and his orchestra played at Frontier Park. The best seat in the rodeo arena allowed you to see "The Daddy of 'em All," for three dollars and a quarter. Sam Stark and Son's, a men's clothing store on 17th street, outfitted those who wanted to dress like cowboys. You could get western pants and a shirt, boots and a cowboy hat for under 30 bucks in those days.

It was the first time I heard of people who would be a significant part of my life in the years to come. Larry Birleffi was the voice of the rodeo, broadcasting the event from Frontier Park on KFBC. I first saw the name of a woman who would become a life-long friend in a newspaper ad. "Shopping Highlights with Margie O'Brien," it read. Margie had a show on KFBC. Five days a week Margie talked to Cheyenne women, providing "First-hand information on new merchandise in Cheyenne and the services of established experts."

The largest shopping center I had ever seen was located not far from my apartment at 8th and Central Avenues, near the Cheyenne airport. There you could eat at a nice café, shop for groceries, drop clothing off for cleaning, visit a chiropractor and a drug store, and drive your car into what we called a "filling station." There a man actually walked out to your car, greeted you, pumped your gas, washed the windshield and checked your oil. Cheyenne's downtown was then the city's commercial center. Fancy restaurants, men's and women's clothing, furniture, and book stores lined the streets. Waldman's could outfit a man with a sports coat for $29.50, a pair of slacks for $6.98, and a dress shirt for $2.50. The Mode O'Day was a women's clothing store. I could buy a fashionable "Puff Taffeta" casual dress for $3.99.

In those days a new, three-bedroom home in Cheyenne sold for twelve thousand five-hundred dollars. A 1950 Studebaker convertible fully equipped with white sidewall tires and a radio went for $1,795.

I quickly grew to like Cheyenne with its tree-lined streets and classic and historic homes near the beautiful Capitol Building. Through a Chi Omega sorority sister, I found a room not far from the Capitol. It was time to go job hunting. Armed with a fresh UW degree with honors, it should have been easier. I'd grown up hearing about the Equality State and how Wyoming had been the first to allow women to vote and elected the first female Governor in the country. It never occurred to me that the state's motto didn't apply to me. I wanted to work in the private accounting sector but quickly realized there was a then impenetrable glass ceiling. Accounting was regarded as a man's profession.

Eventually, I gave up on Cheyenne, traveling to Denver to drop off resumes and job applications. It was no different 100 miles to the south. Each time the message was the same. "Women need not apply." A former professor urged me to take a look at the public sector. So, I applied with the Internal Revenue Service, was hired, and started a fulfilling career that would last more than a quarter of a century.

The IRS of the early 1950s would be unrecognizable to those familiar with the huge federal agency today. Back then, there were no computers. As I took my place at a desk to review tax returns, there was only an old black rotary phone, an adding machine, and a manual typewriter. There were no 1-800 numbers with recorded messages for citizens to call. Instead, they could call us direct, speak to a live human being, even evenings and on Saturdays and get their questions answered.

When I started work, the agency was about to celebrate its 90th anniversary. While the idea of a national income tax had been proposed to pay for the War of 1812, it was first implemented fifty years later by President Abraham Lincoln in 1862. Money was needed to pay the high costs of fighting the Civil War. Lincoln created the Commissioner of Internal Revenue and gave that appointee the job of collecting the nation's first income tax. It had only two levels. Anyone earning between six hundred and ten thousand dollars paid a flat rate of three percent. Those with incomes in excess of ten thousand were taxed at a rate of five percent.

As now, the income tax was not very popular. It was repealed in 1872, reinstated in 1894, and determined by the U.S. Supreme Court to be unconstitutional a year later. The Court found that the income tax violated a provision of the U.S. Constitution requiring direct taxes to be "apportioned among the states." Political leaders like Teddy Roosevelt saw the income tax as a necessary element in the struggle to bridge the gap between the "haves" and the "have-nots."

> "At many stages in the advance of humanity, this conflict between the men who possess more than they have earned and the men who have earned more than they possess is the central condition of progress. In our day, it appears as the struggle of freemen to gain and hold the right of self-government as against the special interests, who twist the methods of free government into machinery for defeating the popular will. At every stage, and under all circumstances, the essence of the struggle is to equalize opportunity, destroy privilege, and give to the life and citizenship of every individual the highest possible value both to himself and to the commonwealth. That is nothing new."[131]

Roosevelt's well-considered arguments notwithstanding, the Supreme Court ordered there would be no income tax unless the Constitution could be amended. It would be left to the state legislatures and the voters. The permanent reinstatement can be attributed to World War I and Wyoming.

Just as Congress needed more revenue to fight the War of 1812 and the Civil War, so it was anticipated as the clouds of a World War gathered on the global horizon. In July of 1909, Congress passed and submitted to the then 46 state legislatures a proposed amendment to the Constitution. Wikipedia's summary of the amendment's history reports, "Opposition to the Sixteenth Amendment was led by establishment Republicans because of their close ties to wealthy industrialists, although not even they were uniformly opposed to the general idea of a permanent income tax." But populists in the Southern and Western states were more favorably disposed to the idea. Alabama, Kentucky, and South Carolina were first to ratify. According to the IRS official account, it was Wyoming that gave the amendment the number of states it needed to complete ratification when its legislators voted affirmatively on February 3, 1913.

Imagine that. It was Wyoming that secured the federal income tax as a part of our lives.

The name of the organization I went to work for in 1951, was the "Bureau of Internal Revenue." Two years later, President Dwight Eisenhower renamed us the "Internal Revenue Service." None of its employees at the massive agency had access to a computer until 1961. When the IRS instituted a toll-free telephone system to provide assistance to taxpayers, the Cheyenne office, where all Wyoming folks filed their returns, was a pilot state.

PRETTY BLOND PASSES WYOMING CPA TEST

In the meantime, I achieved a near-first for Wyoming, breaking one of those glass ceilings. The first people I told were my parents. On January 29, 1956, I wrote a letter to let them know I had passed the exams and was the second-ever female from Wyoming to earn a Certified Public Accountant license. "You know, receiving my certificate seems a little unreal. It's a little difficult to believe that after 8½ years of effort that you've finally achieved what you've been trying to attain. Anyway, it's been quite a struggle. But we finally made it." I told Mom and Dad how I had celebrated by "having my hair trimmed and set. I feel so much better and look a lot better too."

Kirk Knox, a renowned reporter for the *Wyoming Tribune* who would become a close friend, wrote an article about all of this. When it was published in the *Denver Post,* the editor chose what today would be an offensive headline. "Pretty Blond Passes Wyoming CPA Test," it read. Kirk's article went on to report, "With completion of the final phase of examinations in November, Miss Mottonen became the only distaff CPA in the state of Wyoming and one of only three women to ever attain the distinction in this state." Distaff is a term that long ago fell into disuse. It meant anything relating to women. Kirk went on to cite the fact that I was the first and only "female revenue agent to be employed by the federal government in Wyoming." The news story reported my words. "She is not now and has never been treated with condescension by the men with whom she works in the Internal Revenue Service, Miss Mottonen said." That was mostly true.

While I didn't encounter gender discrimination at the IRS, I noticed an occasional raised eyebrow on men who were taken aback to find a woman seated at the table when policy matters were the topic. Fortunately, I was never the target of unwanted sexual advances on the job, though I was aware of many women who were targeted. There were certain men we knew to avoid and all of us women did. I do recall an incident that occurred while I was in Washington, DC for a meeting. I was browsing through an old bookstore in a commercial area not far from the White House. Suddenly I heard a man's voice coming from behind me. "How would you like to come upstairs and go to bed with me?" It was more amusing and pathetic than threatening. I just walked away.

It was during these mid-50s years that the shadow of Joe McCarthy fell hard across Wyoming. Lester Hunt was one of the most popular politicians in the state's history. Though a Democrat in a hugely Republican state, the voters had chosen him to be a legislator, Secretary of State and Governor before his 1948 election to the United States Senate. As Secretary of State, Hunt was credited with the design of the bucking horse license plate. As a wartime Governor, he played a significant role in administering the Selective Service process in his state and undertaking myriad other duties to help the war effort.

Lois sits proudly at her desk as one of the first high ranking IRS employees in the nation.

From the time he arrived in Washington, he and Senator McCarthy locked horns. McCarthy's excessive drinking and womanizing offended the straight-arrow Hunt. But more troubling for the Wyoming lawmaker was McCarthy's demagoguery. McCarthy used his perch in the Senate to ruin the lives of people with half-baked and flat out untrue claims that they were Communists or had Communist leanings. The victims of McCarthyism lost jobs, had their careers ruined along with their reputations, and many resorted to suicide. Senator Hunt openly criticized McCarthy, calling him a drunk and a liar. Hunt introduced legislation to allow McCarthy's victims to sue him for damages. McCarthy vowed to get even with Hunt.

In June of 1953, Senator Hunt's son Buddy was arrested for soliciting homosexual sex in a park across the street from the White House. Powerful Republican leaders attempted to use the episode to force Hunt to resign his Senate seat. The Democrats had a one-vote majority and these Republicans knew that Wyoming's GOP Governor would replace Hunt with one of his own Party, thus shifting control of the Senate. Though Hunt eventually decided not to seek re-election, he refused to resign. As a result, McCarthy announced he planned to hold hearings into an alleged bribe given by a Democratic member of the Senate. Everyone knew he was talking about Hunt. In the early days of Buddy's ordeal, the charges had been dismissed. They were reinstated after Senator Styles Bridges (R-New Hampshire) exerted political influence. With absolutely no evidence, Bridges and another Republican Senator alleged the charges had been dismissed after the arresting officer was paid a bribe. Now that allegation resurfaced and Lester Hunt and his family was about to become the subject of a torturous McCarthy hearing. Hunt decided that would not happen.[132]

On June 9, 1954, the day after McCarthy announced the hearing. Lester Hunt took his own life, firing one rifle shot into his head while seated at his desk in his Senate office.

THIS INCLUDES YOUR WINNINGS OF $50.00

I enjoyed my duties at the IRS and worked hard to let my bosses know how much I appreciated the opportunity. By the early 60s, I had earned a reputation in the IRS. My boss Harry Scribner, district IRS director, wrote that I had "one of the best records of any district in the nation." Mr. Scribner had been impressed that, unlike most applicants for accountancy certification, I had taken the exam only once to become a CPA in Wyoming.

It then happened that Mortimer Caplin, the Commissioner appointed by President John Kennedy to head the IRS, had, at the last minute, to back out of a commitment to appear on the nationally televised game show "What's My Line." The agency quickly decided to send me as his replacement. But I was on a skiing vacation in the Utah mountains and nearly missed the opportunity. Calling several ski resorts and being unable to find me all day on a Thursday before the scheduled program, the IRS took a long shot. Looking in the Salt Lake City phone book, they found a single listing for a "Mottonen." As it turned out it was a relative who knew where I could be found.

By the last Saturday of March 1961, I was in New York City and on Sunday arrived an hour early for the live program. As I took a seat on the stage under the bright TV lights, the panel was introduced. Journalist Dorothy Kilgallen was followed by popular comedian Shelly Berman, actress Arlene Francis, and publisher Bennet Cerf. The host of "What's My Line" was John Daly, who introduced me following a Kelloggs Cereal commercial with the company's classic jingle; "k-e-double L-o-double good, Kellogg's best to you!"

The game began with each contestant asked to "sign in please." Contestants would then write their name on a chalk board. Mr. Daly took time to comment on my penmanship. That would have made my parents proud. Then the questioning started. The studio and TV audience, but not the interrogators, were informed that I was a "Tax collector for the U.S. Government." The panel was allowed to ask "yes" and "no" questions as they endeavored to figure out what the contestant's "line" was. Panel members could continue asking questions until they received a "no." If the panel failed to guess before receiving ten negative responses, the contestant would be declared the winner.

As the game proceeded, one panelist asked if I worked indoors, another inquired whether my job required physical dexterity. Bennet Cerf wanted to know whether I wore a costume. Soon there were six "no" responses with only four to go. Then Cerf guessed it. "Is a lovely lady like you involved in collecting taxes?"

I received a check for "your winnings of $50.00." Leaving the studio and walking along those busy New York streets, I was surprised to be stopped by New Yorkers who recognized me from my altogether brief appearance on national television. I soon returned to Cheyenne to a front-page story about the show.

I GUESS THAT IS THE WAY IT HAD TO BE

In July of 1961, I learned that Uncle Ray Matson had died at the Wyoming State Hospital (WSH). Although the Hospital was aware that I was Ray's only relative in Wyoming and had my address, they initially told me nothing about Uncle Ray's death. Instead, the hospital staff sent a telegram to Ray's sister in Washington State. It contained none of the details, but "merely said that Mr. Matson had died and requested instructions concerning funeral arrangements."[133] It wasn't the first time the State Hospital failed to inform the family of significant events occurring over the many years since Ray was initially admitted.

In the early years of Wyoming as a Territory and as a state, the state was divided between five counties. Legislators divided key institutions among them. From east to west, Laramie County was awarded the State Capitol at Cheyenne, Albany County received the University of Wyoming, located in Laramie, the State Prison went to Rawlins in Carbon County, the State Miner's hospital was established in Sweetwater County at Rock Springs, and the Wyoming State Hospital, which was then called the "Wyoming

Insane Asylum," was built in Uinta County in the small town of Evanston.

Evanston is named for James Evans, who surveyed part of the Union Pacific's eastern route through Wyoming, which means he may never have actually seen the town named for him.[134] The Territorial Legislature voted to establish the Wyoming Insane Asylum there in 1887. A $30,000 appropriation bought a 100-acre plot on a hill overlooking Evanston from its southern edge and paid for the construction of the hospital's first building. For years, it has been said the place is haunted.

> *"A single sheet hangs in a room window facing the interstate. Authorities thought it necessary to place there because of repeated sightings of a young girl reliving her death, caused by hanging, every night. Many people have born witness to this disturbing occurrence. There is no power and lights will be on at night, a rocker will be rocking, howling noises, strange floating lights are all reported."*[135]

As the asylum was being built, my ancestors were immigrating to the United States where they would eventually find themselves in Wyoming. They could not have anticipated how the hospital at Evanston would become a haunting part of our family history.

The site and the operation of the facility was largely influenced by social reformer Dorothea Dix and a Pennsylvanian who was at the vanguard of new ideas about treating mentally ill patients. Thomas Kirkbride was a Quaker physician. He was an advocate for providing treatment with an expectation of curing the patient's illness as opposed to simply warehousing them. He believed, "The very concept of moral treatment was synonymous with the creation of a specific environment that would facilitate recovery."[136] In order to help the mentally ill recover, Kirkbride encouraged mental hospitals to secure sites of at least 100 acres in a serene country setting. This mode of treatment encouraged care providers to house patients "in comfortable and pleasant environs" where they would be "treated with kindness and respect, and encouraged through rational discussions to regain their mental balance."[137]

That was the "Kirkbride Model," which had been the driving force in mental health residential treatment since the middle of the 19th century when a consensus began to develop around the notion that the seriously mentally ill should not be treated in their community, but in asylums. Kirkbride, it was said, "rationalized prevailing psychiatric beliefs into a coherent, consistent, and unified body of thought."

It was in that context that the people of Wyoming built the hospital at Evanston. However, the thing about theories of how to treat the mentally ill is that they are forever evolving. The challenging complexities of mental illness are such that success rates are low and therefore, the experts are on a constant search for what works. Between the time the asylum was built at Evanston and the time my Uncle Ray Matson became a patient there, psychiatrists continually altered "the basic foundation of their specialty."[138] In the process, "They identified new careers outside of institutions, articulated novel theories and therapies." Among them was the lobotomy.

ONE FLEW OVER THE CUCKOO NEST

My memories of Uncle Ray begin with the delightful fishing trips our family enjoyed. Other memories are of visiting him on the grounds of the Wyoming State Hospital. I always associated his mental difficulties with the fact that only he among his brothers was excluded from military service during World War II. Ray had a large red birthmark we called "a raspberry." It may well have been a vascular tumor known as a capillary hemangioma. These tumors are formed by a large number of blood vessels near the surface of the skin. Even a slight incident can cause catastrophic bleeding. Military medical gatekeepers would have had sufficient reason for deciding he was unfit for combat. Therefore, as his brothers and most of the men in Rock Springs answered the call, Ray was left behind.

Today it may be difficult to imagine the stigma suffered by adult men who walked the streets back home while most of their family and friends were off fighting the war. There was a moral imperative about the war that instilled a deep sense of patriotism. Along with it came an expectation that all men should serve. Those who could not march off to the war felt a sense of being judged. Perhaps it was that sense that caused Ray's behavior to lead someone to believe he needed to be institutionalized.

The truth is that I have no idea how it came to pass that Uncle Ray found himself a patient of the State Hospital. Back then no one spoke of those things. Today, there is no one left to ask. The records that exist are confidential and legally beyond reach. In any event, Ray was admitted to the Wyoming State Hospital on December 11, 1949. But for a six-month "parole" in 1950, Patient No. 4354 was there for the last 12 years of his life, which ended in 1961.

While Ray was hospitalized, his mother Hilma died. Ray was not allowed to leave the hospital long enough to attend her funeral service. On March 26, 1950, he wrote to his brothers and sister.

> *"I'm very disappointed that I didn't get to attend mother's funeral, as I would have liked to have had a last look at her before she was put away, but evidently it wasn't in the cards to be that way, Well, it's nothing unusual for me to get a raw deal from one end or the other."*

A clue to why Ray was hospitalized is found in a letter that remains among my family papers. It was written by Ray. It is in his hand in now fading ink. The date Ray wrote at the top of the first page is difficult to read, but I believe it says the letter was written on August 28, 1951. If so, it would have been some 20 months after his admission and a little more than eight months after he returned to the hospital after his August, 1950, parole. That parole ended with Uncle Ray's return to Evanston on January 12, 1951.

In the letter Ray lamented,

"I wish I had lived differently. I probably wouldn't be in the predicament I am in today. But I guess that is the way it had to be, so there isn't any use in crying over or regretting the past, only except to wait and see what the future has in store for one, and hope best if there is anything of that sort."

Part of what the future had in store for my Uncle was a "surgical procedure that involved severing the nerve fibers of the frontal lobes of the brain." A lobotomy produced effects that were "irreversible and the outcome not always predictable."[139] Jack Nicholson, in his role as McMurphy, received a lobotomy in "One Flew Over the Cuckoo's Nest." It was done to get him under control and, per the popular book and movie, rendered him compliant. President Kennedy's sister Rosemary was given a lobotomy which according to an NPR report, rendered her "inert and unable to speak more than a few words."[140] NPR said lobotomies were used for people with certain diagnoses.

"Tension, apprehension, anxiety, depression, insomnia, suicidal ideas, delusions, hallucinations, crying spells, melancholia, obsessions, panic states, disorientation, psychalgesia (pains of psychic origin), nervous indigestion and hysterical paralysis."

Ray's family didn't know whether Ray suffered from any of those conditions. The doctors never told us. Likewise, we were never told that Uncle Ray was given a lobotomy in the early weeks of 1951, which would have been soon after he returned to the hospital following his unsuccessful parole. To my knowledge, none of his family was consulted before the surgery nor were any informed of the outcome. My father would have never learned of Ray's lobotomy had he not visited Ray shortly after the procedure had been carried out. Hospital officials attempted to stall father from seeing Ray but finally a doctor arrived and explained that he had been lobotomized. Father found his brother in terrible condition. I don't believe Ray ever fully recovered.

Unbelievably, neither was the family informed of Uncle Ray's last illness after which he died alone because of the hospital's failure to inform members of the family who would have wanted to be with him in his final hours. After receiving the telegram from the Hospital informing her of Ray's death, his elderly sister called on me to help make final arrangements. When she called me, I called the hospital to find what had happened to my Uncle. I was told only that I should contact the undertaker. I did.

But, as Uncle Ray would say, "I guess that is the way it had to be, so there isn't any use in crying over or regretting the past."

I NEVER GOT OVER THE EXTREME
SADNESS I FELT THEN

On September 25, 1961, I was one of the thousands of people flocking to the Cheyenne airport to get a glimpse of John F. Kennedy, the President of the United States. It was a typical fall day in Wyoming, clear skies, temperatures in the mid-70s. We all cheered loudly as Air Force One landed at the small airport. The cheers grew even louder as the historic aircraft's door opened and the President, accompanied by Wyoming's U.S. Senator Gale McGee, descended the stairs and strolled to a platform where the President delivered a fine speech. The President was tanned and handsome. Who could have predicted that within two months, this man would be dead?

It always seemed our state held a special place in the President's heart. Wyoming played a key role in JFK's election to the Presidency. In those days, there were few presidential primaries and the nomination was left largely to political bosses and influential party members. It was they, through a series of maneuvers, some in smoke-filled backrooms and others in the open, who would piece together enough delegate votes to win the party's nomination. The 1960 Democratic National Convention was in Los Angeles. Because of its small size, Wyoming had only

15 of the 1521 delegates, fewer than one percent. However, the roll was called alphabetically when the question was whether the Party would nominate JFK or Lyndon Johnson for President. When Wyoming's turn eventually rolled around, Kennedy needed 11 more votes. Wyoming gave him 15 and Kennedy went on from there to barely defeat Richard Nixon the following November.

That's why the President was in Wyoming less than two months before Lee Harvey Oswald assassinated him on the streets of Dallas. I had been in Dallas for an IRS training a few days before the tragedy. As I looked back in the days that followed, it seemed to me the air there was tense and hate-filled. I returned to Dallas in December of 1963. A few of us visited Dealey Plaza and stared up at the window from which the assassin fired his deadly volley. I never got over the extreme sadness I felt then.

AN ANGRY INSURGENCY OVERCAME MUCH OF THE IGNORANCE AND MISUNDERSTANDING CREATED BY DECADES OF DENIAL AND OBFUSCATION

It was the late 60s when the coal mines my father left years earlier came back to haunt him. The black lung disease lingering in him for many years made an appearance. As it happened to so many, it now happened to my father. The retired miners had already been put through the wringer, fighting battles with well-funded company doctors and researchers who were determined to deny the disease even existed, much less in the bodies of men for whom they might have financial responsibility.

It was the annual meeting for the Colorado Medical Society. Its President, H.A. Lemen, a Denver University professor of medicine, presented a paper on a disease contracted by one of his patients. The patient exhibited symptoms that included a "harassing cough," "care-worn expressions," and expectoration of as much as a pint a day of a liquid with a "decidedly inky appearance." Lemen was sensational about making his point as he read, "The sentence I am reading was written with this fluid. The pen used has never been in ink."[141]

Thus, began a long and winding road for miners and their advocates as they worked until 1969 to persuade the Congress and the President that "black lung disease" was real. State and national governments had never accepted the idea that miners deserved occupational protection. Certainly, they paid safety lip service but were never far from blaming the miners for injuries and death in the mines. The government was always more interested in what came out of the mines than the workers who brought it out even though coal technology in the years before, during and after Nestor worked the mines was dependent on the hands and arms of miners.

Alan Derickson's 1998 book, *Black Lung-Anatomy of a Public Health Disaster,* chronicles the fight miners waged against their government, their employers, and faux medical science. The latter claimed at one point that the mines were healthy environments, that coal mines presented an environment inhospitable to infection."[142] It was said that as the air passed through the mines, the bacteria fell to the ground and was, thereby, purified before it reached the nostrils of the miners.

So certain was the medical science, that by 1905, 200 medical doctors responded to a questionnaire from the editor of the *Journal of the American Medical Association,* with three out of four agreeing that coal miners were not susceptible to tuberculosis.[143] A decade later, with father still laboring in the mines and still breathing in the coal dust that would kill him more than half a century later, the industry proudly proclaimed "the atmosphere of the mine is now vindicated even though its healthfulness has not yet been extolled."[144]

The science blurred with the business of coal mining and then with the politics of worker protection. Wyoming has a long tradition of caring little about worker safety and the legislature is determined to make sure it continues. Even as this book is written, Wyoming ranks 2nd in the nation for tolerating workplace fatalities. Lawmakers serve the interests of employers in such a craven manner that this tradition is a hallmark of working in Wyoming now as it was when medical findings contrary to those of the industry were swept under the rug while sick miners continued to become disabled and die. Union leaders, especially at the local level, could not so easily ignore the matter. They "remained face to face with a sizeable contingent of dyspneic men (exhibiting labored breathing) struggling to stay on the job or struggling to survive after becoming too debilitated to work."[145]

By the end of the 1960s, "an angry insurgency overcame much of the ignorance and misunderstanding created by decades of denial and obfuscation."[146] Having fought losing battles in the state legislatures of the coal mining states where politicians were owned by the industry, the miners and their unions turned to Congress. In 1969, Congress at long last enacted the Federal Coal Mine Health and Safety Act. It provided compensation for miners suffering from black lung disease.

It was too late for Nestor Mottonen. He died of what his doctor diagnosed as black lung disease in 1971, without ever seeing a dime in compensation. In May 1972, Wyoming Senator Gale W. McGee, to whom Nestor's widow had gone for help in obtaining benefits under the 1969 law, informed Cecelia her claim for Black Lung benefits had been approved. Months later, the U.S. Government sent her a check for $1200.

SHE HAS BROUGHT HONOR TO BOTH THE
INSTITUTION AND HERSELF THROUGH
CONTRIBUTIONS IN THE FIELD OF PUBLIC SERVICE

The United States celebrated its Bicentennial in 1976. I had cause to celebrate that year for another reason. In September, I received a letter from Mike Johns, the Executive Director of Alumni Relations at the University of Wyoming. "On behalf of the Alumni Association," it read, "I want to extend our congratulations for your selection as a recipient of the University of Wyoming Distinguished Alumni Award."

The citation said I had "brought honor to both the institution and herself through contributions in the field of public service." It noted my work for the IRS and nominations for the annual Federal Women's Award and Federal Civil Servant of the Year in 1973, as well as the Ford Foundation Fellowship. It noted that I was the first woman in government to become president of the American Women's Society of CPAs and founder and first president of the Wyoming Chapter of the American Society of Women Accountants. It gave me great pride that UW also recognized my service to my alma mater. I had been chair of the Advisory Council at UW's College of Commerce and received the College of Commerce and Industry's outstanding alumni award earlier that year. As the University's president Dr. William Carlson handed me the award at the October 2nd All-Alumni Luncheon following UW's homecoming parade, my thoughts were with my parents who had sacrificed so much so that I could attend the school and for teaching me that I was expected to give back to the community.

THE FIRST WOMAN APPOINTED TO A TOP-LEVEL POSITION IN THE INTERNAL REVENUE SERVICE

I served the IRS faithfully for a quarter of a century and amassed a personnel file overflowing with awards and letters from every level of the IRS, including Douglas Dillon, JFK's Secretary of the Treasury, recognizing what he called my "exemplary service." Even so, it was a very bureaucratic change in agency policy that ended my career there. On June 30, 1979, I retired from IRS. The agency implemented a personnel rule requiring all of its employees be readily able to accept relocation to any office in the country. In addition to my IRS duties, I was by then also caring for my mother who was living with me in Cheyenne. I simply could not commit to the new policy and so chose to retire.

I had been a revenue agent, audit supervisor, returns program manager, and chief of the collection and taxpayer services division. The IRS lauded my work as "a leader in many professional organizations." Bob G. Hughes, the IRS District Director at the time of my retirement, said I had been "the first woman appointed to a top-level position in the Internal Revenue Service." I was likewise the first woman in government to ever serve as president of the American Women's Society of CPAs and founded the first Wyoming chapter of the organization in 1970.

My career with the IRS had ended. Another door soon opened and I found an altogether new career path working for the Wyoming Department of Education as its "Sex Equity Coordinator."

---

131   Eric Black, "Teddy Roosevelt's Attack on Excessive Concentration of Wealth, https://www.minnpost.com/eric-black-ink/2011/12/teddy-roosevelts-attack-excessive-concentration-wealth, accessed May 4, 2017

132   Rodger McDaniel, *Dying for Joe McCarthy's Sins: The Suicide of Wyoming Senator Lester Hunt,* Wordsworth Publishing (2013); all information in this section came from this book.

133   July 18, 1961 letter from Lois Mottonen to Wyoming State Hospital Administrator Dr. William Karns, personal collection of Mottonen.

134   Barbara Allen Bogart, "Evanston, Wyoming" http://www.wyohistory.org/encyclopedia/evanston-wyoming

135   "Haunted Places in Wyoming" http://theshadowlands.net/places/wyoming.htm.

136   Gerald N. Grob, *The Mad Among Us: A History of Care of America's Mentally Ill,* Free Press (1994), 70.

137   Barbara Bogart, *"The Hospital on the Hill,"* Annals of Wyoming, Vol. 79, No. 1, (Winter 2007), 2.

138   Grob, *The Mad Among Us,* 130.

139   Grob, *The Mad Among Us,* 183.

140   "My Lobotomy," http://www.npr.org/templates/story/story.php?storyId=5014565 accessed June 3, 2017.

141   Derickson, *Black Lung,* 1.

142   Derickson, *Black Lung,* 46.

143   *Journal of the American Medical Association,* November 21, 1905, 45.

144   *Coal Trade Journal,* September 7, 1904, 651.

145   Derickson, *Black Lung,* 113.

146   Derickson, *Black Lung,* 143.

CHAPTER TEN

WE HAD GREAT SUCCESS DESPITE RELIGIOUS AND
POLITICAL ATTITUDES NOT FAVORABLE TO WOMEN

As I opened a new career path at the Wyoming Department of Education, I was given the responsibility of leading the agency's campaign to confront gender, racial, and other forms of bias in education. In 1976, Congress mandated that every state appoint a full-time sex equity coordinator. I was excited to be the first to fill that role in Wyoming where I knew it was so badly needed. During Congressional debate, U.S. Representative Patsy Mink of Hawaii said:

> *"Discrimination against women in education is one of the most insidious forms of prejudice extant in our nation. Few people realize the extent to which our society is denied full use of our human resources because of this type of discrimination."*[147]

Congresswoman Shirley Chisholm, an African-American woman who ran for President in 1972, and whom I had the pleasure of meeting during these years, added:

> *"For the life of me, I can't understand how we can continue to be so uptight about whether a person wears a dress or a pair of pants, as to whether that person can use their God-given talents to make whatever contributions they can to this country."*

I remembered when one of my high school teachers was as uptight about whether a person was wearing a dress or a pair of pants. I felt the sting of bias first as a high school student in Rock Springs, confronted by a male physics teacher who didn't think girls belonged in his class. I remembered the sting of bias when I encountered the doors closed to women in the accounting community of Cheyenne. The opportunity to be a part of an effort to confront this issue excited me. However, the program didn't excite state legislators quite so much. During the 1977 session of the legislature, the Appropriations Committee one day zeroed out all of the funding for the sex equity coordinator. The next day, after the Governor made it known to them that federal law required the program to be funded with the money Washington provided, the funding was restored. Nonetheless, these Equality State legislators had made clear we'd have to work through their disdain for what we were doing.

I was proud to be able to work with a group of courageous women and men who made the program work well despite opposition from the state legislature. They included Verlyn Velle, Julie Uhlmann, Abel Benavidez, James Lamphrect, Judy Kishman, Shirley Humphrey (who later served in the Wyoming Legislature), Karen Milmont, and Teri Wigert.

One of my jobs was to publish a quarterly newsletter titled "*Wyoming Equity*." It provided teachers, administrators, parents and policymakers a wide variety of information resources on the extent to which teachers and students were negatively impacted by inequities inherent in the educational system.

Wyoming Equity shined a light on issues such as gender impact on testing, sex bias in classrooms, sexual harassment of students, inequity in physical education and sports, and the gender gap in professional opportunities for both teachers and students. Writers whose work was presented in the publication bravely confronted the racism, misogyny, and homophobia at a time when few other Wyoming people were willing to discuss those matters.

I was honored to have been recognized as an "Equity Pioneer" by the National Alliance of Partnerships in Equity in 1998, after I had retired from the Department of Education. In their recognition, I was quoted. "We had great success despite religious and political attitudes not favorable to women." That was true even though those were tough conversations even 15 years after the passage of the Civil Rights Act of 1964. They still are half a century later in a state that has never fully lived its motto. The Equality State has never been an especially tolerant place for those who are not white, male, Christian heterosexuals.

NO INDIANS, NO MEXICANS, NO NEGROES

In spite of, maybe because of never having had many black people or other minorities among its citizenry, Wyoming long had a problem accepting them. Neither has the state been accountable to women. The state motto may have referred to allowing women to vote though it never extended to giving women the rights to much else. The motto certainly did not assure non-white citizens of much of anything. Even before statehood, the Territorial Legislature enacted an anti-miscegenation statute prohibiting marriages between Caucasians and "a person of one-eighth or more negro, asiatic (sic), or Mongolian blood." Such marriages were deemed felonies. It was repealed in 1882, and reenacted in 1913, before being repealed one last time in 1965.

Lois accepts her Distinguished Alumnus Award from University of Wyoming President William Carlson.

The same legislature passed laws mandating segregated schools.[148] Historian Regan Joy Kaufman noted that although there is no evidence any Wyoming school district used the statute's authority to segregate classrooms, "Wyoming, a state far removed from the South, was hardly void of racial discrimination." Though not used, these statutes remained on the books and available until after the U.S. Supreme Court found school segregation in violation of the Constitution in 1954's *Brown v. Board of Education* ruling.

Two years ahead of me, twenty-three-year-old Harriet

State Senator Elizabeth Byrd presides over the Senate. *Photo courtesy of the Wyoming State Archives*

Elizabeth Byrd graduated from the University of Wyoming in 1949. She was black. She was also imminently qualified to teach. Unlike the experiences of colleges in the South, Wyoming Governors didn't have to stand in the doorway to block blacks from attending. They could study at UW and earn a degree, but that was the end of the road. With her degree in hand, Mrs. Byrd applied for a teaching job in Cheyenne. The State Superintendent of Public Instruction refused her application. Whites, it was said, didn't want black teachers disciplining their children. Thus, Wyoming did not hire "Negro teachers."[149] Despite her University of Wyoming degree, it was another decade, 1959, before Mrs. Byrd could get a classroom-teaching job. She later served with distinction in the Wyoming Legislature from 1981 until 1992, sponsoring a number of bills targeting discrimination.

As a state Senator, Mrs. Byrd pushed through the legislation designating Martin Luther King's January birthday a state holiday. Wyoming passed it reluctantly, one of the last states to do so, and the legislature itself has never honored the day or respected Dr. King enough to take the day off. Indeed, the history of the King holiday includes even another shameful episode. In 1972, Michael Tyler, a high school student at Cheyenne Central, asked the principal if students could have an assembly to recognize Rev. King four years after the murder of the civil rights icon. He was told yes, but student-faculty attendance had to be voluntary and the event held after school hours.

In order to publicize the "voluntary" event, Tyler and other African-American students distributed flyers. They read, "If you're Black and proud, Brown and smart, White and concerned, urge your homeroom teacher to allow your class to attend the Martin Luther King Day assembly." The assembly was a success, well attended, but Tyler and others paid a dear, though unwarranted, price. He and nine other students were suspended for distributing written material in violation of some innocuous school policy. Tyler, like Mrs. Byrd, overcame it all, leaving the "Equality State in the rear view mirror and going on the graduate *summa cum laude* from Morehouse College before graduating from Harvard Law School. He now enjoys a successful career at a major Atlanta law firm.[150] The bigotry of the state has always come with the high cost of losing some of the best young, home-grown minds. Alas, so few of the state's elite ever make the connection though they constantly moan the departure of so many of our youth.

One reason Liz Byrd may have successfully broken the color barrier in 1959 was the outrage of two influential white men who witnessed blatant racism at a Cheyenne restaurant two years earlier.

> *"Two prominent Wyomingites watched as an African-American serviceman and his spouse seated themselves in the little cafe at Cheyenne's Plains Hotel in 1954. The couple sipped water and read the menus. Suddenly a waitress jumped from her station and snatched away the menus. The manager entered the scene and ushered the two African-Americans out of the restaurant. Teno Roncalio and Dr. Francis Barrett discussed the shameful incident they had witnessed."*[151]

Roncalio, who came of age, as did I, in the ethnic, racial, and culturally diverse Rock Springs, later served 10 years as Wyoming's Congressman, and was then Chairman of the Wyoming Democratic Party. Dr. Barrett was the son of U.S. Senator Frank Barrett. Each found what they had witnessed to be unacceptable and they were determined to right the wrong. They walked the story up Capitol Avenue to Governor Milward Simpson. Governor Simpson, moved by what he had heard, proposed the legislature pass a civil rights bill drafted by Roncalio. The law was enacted in 1957. "No person of good deportment shall be denied the right of life, liberty, pursuit of happiness, or the necessities of life because of race, color, creed, or national origin."[152] It seemed Wyoming might be in the process of reforming its views of blacks. Even so, seven years later two out of Wyoming's three members of Congress, including now U.S.

Senator Milward Simpson, voted against the Civil Rights Act of 1964.

Across the nation, those who had been fighting for civil rights thought their time had come. But state governments, including Wyoming's, had an ugly history to live down. It had been not much more than a generation since lynching blacks was at its historic zenith in Wyoming.[153] Some of those who participated were likely still living their lives in the Cowboy State when Congress finally got around to enacting laws against lynching.

Historian Todd Guenther documents the arrival of the first slaves in Wyoming in 1863. In 1864, the first of them was lynched at Fort Halleck near Elk Mountain. A man known only as "Asa," was one of them. He was owned by the Fort's surgeon and was accused of "insulting and kissing a white girl." The surgeon reported his slave's demise casually, gleefully writing in his diary, "Asa killed by the boys of Co. D for committing rape upon little girl just 12 years old-Dissected him-exciting time."

Wyomingites had occasion for many more such "exciting" times in the years ahead. "Lynching became 'a tool for white Wyomingites to assert racial authority." Guenther's 2009 article documents numerous Wyoming lynchings of African Americans. When a black Laramie jail inmate was accused of an improbable act of "slashing a young white woman employed at the jail when she refused his amorous advances," the *Laramie Boomerang* didn't complain that the lynching took place with no due process but that the Laramie residents who shot at the victim many times, hit him only once. The newspaper said they were "poor shots."

The decade of the 1910s was when most Wyoming lynchings occurred. Many of those who were lynched were stereotypically accused of sex crimes against white women. The accusers needed no evidence. Rumors sufficed. Frank Wigfall, described by the *Wyoming Tribune,* in an October 12, 1912 report as "a big negro with a face more like a beast than a man," was in prison for "rape and assault." He was lynched there after guards gave a group of inflamed white inmates their blessing to hang him.

By the middle of that decade, Guenther says the white majority in Wyoming, then as now, was deeply concerned about the "hordes of minorities" who "were sweeping over the Equality State." The Census Bureau's statistics demonstrate their fears were unfounded but that fact didn't reduce the fear of whites or the threat to people of color. The lynching continued. Guilty or innocent, blacks could find no protection in the Constitution or the state motto. Guenther asserted, "A black man's life wasn't worth much in the Equality State."

Joel Woodson, an African-American Union Pacific employee was lynched in December 1918. A mob of Rock Springs citizens dragged Woodson from a jail cell where he was being held in connection with murder allegations. He was taken to the UP depot and lynched. *Photo courtesy of the Sweetwater County Historical Museum*

Between 1910 and 1920, five Wyoming blacks were lynched, a per capita rate higher than the national average, and 123 times that of Mississippi. The Ku Klux Klan organized in several Wyoming communities, including, according Guenther's chronicles, Sheridan, Casper, Torrington, Riverton, Shoshoni, and Lander. "All across the state, businesses posted signs in their front windows saying, 'No Indians, No Mexicans, No Negroes." It was 1919 before the Wyoming legislature passed a resolution condemning the mob violence but the racism persisted.

I CAN'T LET YOU MARRY THIS GIRL ON WYOMING'S MONEY

Wyoming's struggle with racial equality was on full display years before I worked at the Department of Education in what is known as "the Black 14 incident." It was October 1969, long after Wyoming should have known better. Wyoming had an outstanding and nationally ranked football team. On the eve of an October 18 game against arch-rival Brigham Young University, a Church of Latter Day Saints (Mormons) school, 14 UW players asked head coach Lloyd Eaton if they could wear black arm bands during the game as a way of protesting the Mormon church's exclusion of African Americans from the LDS priesthood. Without bothering to answer the question, Coach Eaton summarily dismissed all 14 players from the team, ending their scholarships and their UW educations.

Eaton had previously exhibited traits that could have been seen as racist. One of the 14 was Mel Hamilton. He remembered an earlier encounter with Eaton during a 2013 oral history interview with historian Phil White. Hamilton had decided to get married "and I went [to] Red Jacoby, (Glenn "Red" Jacoby was UW athletic director from 1946 until 1973) who was the athletic director—keep in mind the athletic director's in charge of all coaches—and he told me—I went to him and said I wanted to get okay for married student housing, because I was going to marry this girl. He knew she was white. He said "Mel, that'd be fine, fine, why don't you go tell Lloyd [Coach Lloyd Eaton] to write the papers up.

"And as I was going into the Field House and Coach Eaton was coming down, we met on the steps and I said, "Just the man I'm looking for, here's what Mr. Jacoby said, I need for you to write up the papers." [He said,] "No way, Mel. That's not gonna happen." I said, "What do you mean?" [And he said,] "I can't let you marry this girl on Wyoming's money, the people of Wyoming's money."[154]

Eaton was talking about "the good old boys," a group of influential, high dollar supporters of the school's athletic programs who would find a black man married to a white woman offensive. Eaton was likely worried about those same white folks when his players told him of their plans to protest BYU's racial policies. In effect, the head coach said, "That's not gonna happen. I can't let you wear those arm bands on Wyoming's money." All 14 were kicked off the team and lost their scholarships overnight.

As a result, a great debate erupted throughout the state with politicians and most citizens taking sides, most often the side of Coach Eaton and supporting him with racial taunts aimed at the student athletes. Without those 14 athletes on the field, Wyoming still defeated BYU 40-7 with at least one fan waving a Confederate flag in the stands. The Cowboys won their next game too. But that was it. They lost the remainder of their 1969 games and all but one the following year. Lloyd Eaton retired and eventually left Wyoming, though the stain of his racism never did.

To date, half a century later, the University has never apologized to these men. But the state has doubled down on its

Branding Iron Confederate Flag
Photo courtesy of the American Heritage Center, University of Wyoming.

attitude toward minorities. Wyoming held out till nearly all others had declared Martin Luther King's birthday a holiday and then reluctantly passed a diluted "Martin Luther King-Equality Day" law with no recognition of the irony. By 2018, Wyoming remained one of five states unwilling to enact hate crimes legislation.

WHEN THE PARENTS DID RETURN RICHARD
JAHNKE SHOT SIX TIMES THROUGH THE GARAGE
DOOR, WITH FOUR OF THE SLUGS STRIKING THE
FATHER AND KILLING HIM ALMOST INSTANTLY.

Not long after I started my work at the Department of Education, Cheyenne made the national news as a result of one of the darkest incidents in the state's history. The case, involving the murder of an IRS employee I never knew, stirred a great debate in educational and child welfare circles.

It was a typically cold evening in November as Richard Jahnke arrived with his wife Maria at their home in North Cheyenne. Richard got out of the car to open the garage door. A shotgun blast tore through the cold air and ripped Richard's body. He was killed instantly. Maria screamed and ran from the car to see what had happened. She saw her 16-year-old son holding the shotgun. Richie ran into the house and retrieved his sister Deborah and they fled. Once apprehended, the two juveniles faced murder charges in a Laramie County District Court.

As the trial began, it was all we talked about at work and among friends. The evidence provided a window into the lives too many young people live. Maria was a battered wife. Her two children were systematically abused by the father they decided must die. At the trial, it was Richie who gave up the long-held family secrets. His father had not only beaten Maria and Richie, he had been sexually violating his daughter for years.

He pushed my sister against the wall and to discipline
her he'd grope her breasts. I once saw him reach into
my sister's pants and feel around. Dad would tuck

Deborah into bed; once I looked into the room and saw him lying on top of my sister."[155]

In deciding against Deborah on appeal the Wyoming Supreme Court, the majority opinion included this set of facts:

"Following years of both physical and psychological abuse of the children by the father, matters came to a head on the evening of November 16, 1982. After an altercation between the deceased father, Richard Chester Jahnke, and Deborah Jahnke's brother, Richard John Jahnke, which included the father's striking the brother with his fists, the Jahnke children's parents went out to dinner. While they were gone Richard made elaborate preparations for confronting his father. These preparations included loading firearms and placing them at several "back-up" locations throughout the house; putting the family pets in the basement for their safety; and waiting in a darkened garage with a shotgun loaded with slugs for the parents to return. When the parents did return Richard Jahnke shot six times through the garage door, with four of the slugs striking the father and killing him almost instantly."[156]

It fell to Governor Ed Herschler to commute the children's sentences to keep them out of long prison terms.

WIND RIVER RESERVATION

It was during these years at the Wyoming Department of Education that I first came to know there was a Third World Nation within the boundaries of the State of Wyoming. The Wind River Reservation (WRR) is comprised of chunks of Fremont and Hot Springs counties in central Wyoming. It was established as a way of reigning in two Indian tribes from the vast territories that were once theirs. It is home to the Northern Arapaho and Eastern Shoshone.

When people of the Wind River Reservation weren't being

ignored by the government, they were being deceived. WRR boundaries were originally established by the 1863 Fort Bridger Treaty to include 44 million acres across parts of Wyoming, Idaho, Utah, and Colorado. After decades of taking, the Reservation now covers less than 3 million acres with ongoing boundary disputes threatening them.

The Reservation is a sad monument to the neglect of Native Americans. The conditions are imaginable only if compared to how non-Native people live in the same state. Compare conditions on the Wind River to those of any of Wyoming's 23 counties. A 2016 report titled "In the Heart of Wyoming is Indian Country" describes contemporary life on the Wind River Reservation and allows us to make the comparisons. Funded by the Wyoming Office of Multicultural Health, the report was sponsored by the Wind River Advocacy Center, Wyoming Department of Health, and Wyoming Association of Churches (now known as the Wyoming Interfaith Network).

U.S. and Wyoming citizens living on that Reservation suffer an average life expectancy of 20% fewer years than those living in any other county. Cancer rates there are 20% higher than any of the other counties, where chronic liver disease was diagnosed 90% more often. The infant mortality, that is the rate at which parents watch their newborn children die, is more than 100% higher than in all the other Wyoming counties. Hundreds of Reservation families live without adequate heat during Wyoming's winters. The median household income is half of other Wyoming counties and a quarter of the poorest households earn less than $9,000 a year, leaving nearly two-thirds of them below the poverty line?

Native Americans did not become U.S. Citizens until 1924, the year before Wyoming elected its first and only female Governor and more than half a century after Wyoming's Territorial legislature gave women the right to vote. So, when the state adopted its motto, it was not likely envisioned that Indians would be included in any understanding of equality in the Equality State. The federal Indian Citizenship Act of 1924 didn't change that, nor has anything else since. Native Americans remain second class citizens in Wyoming despite the fact that the U.S. Supreme Court long ago held that the government has a moral and legal responsibility to care for Native Americans.

---

147   Hearings before the Special Subcommittee on Education of the Committee on Education and Labor, U.S. House of Representatives, Second Session of Congress, June 17, 1970, 433.

148   Reagan Joy Kaufman, "Discrimination in the 'Equality State'-Black-White Relations in Wyoming History, *Annals of Wyoming (Winter 2005)*, 13.

149   Guenther, "The List of 'Good Negroes," 27-29.

150   King's legacys 'indeed worthy of celebration," *Wyoming Tribune-Eagle*, January 16, 2018, 1

151   Kim Ibach and William Howard Moore, "The Emerging Civil Rights Movement: The 1957 Wyoming Public Accommodations Statute as a Case Study" http://www.uwyo.edu/robertshistory/civil_rights_movement.htm, accessed March 16, 2015.

152   Larson, *The History of Wyoming*, 1st Edition, 524.

153   Unless otherwise indicated, the information in this section is derived mostly from an Annals of Wyoming article appearing in the Spring of 2009, written by Todd Guenther and titled "The List of Good Negroes'-African American Lynchings in the Equality State."

154   Phil White, Former University of Wyoming Football Player Mel Hamilton on his life and the Black 14, http://www.wyohistory.org/oral-histories/former-university-wyoming-football-player-mel-hamilton-his-life-and-black-14

155   Leo Janos, On a Windswept Wyoming Prairie An Abused Son Kills a Father to Bring Peace to a Family," People Magazine, March 7, 1983, http://people.com/archive/on-a-windswept-wyoming-prairie-an-abused-son-kills-a-father-to-bring-peace-to-a-family-vol-19-no-9/, accessed June 6, 2017.

156   Jahnke v. State, 1984 WY 114, 692 P.2d 911 (1984).

CHAPTER ELEVEN

WHAT DOES EQUALITY HAVE TO DO WITH IT?

Governor Stan Hathaway, in a moment of genuine candor, once said, "Wyoming is a great place to live if you can find a job." Other than the first months after college as I struggled unsuccessfully to break Cheyenne's glass ceiling among private accountancy firms, I have been fortunate to always be able to find fulfilling work at fair wages. I've seen many others, particularly women, who have not been so fortunate.

I've also been fortunate to have had the financial wherewithal to repay the assistance I received by helping today's struggling students get an education. I didn't do it alone and I am not sure anyone else ever did either.

There's always been a sort of "pull yourself up by your bootstraps" attitude in this state even among those who can't afford bootstraps. From where I sit, it's clear the attitude starts at the top. Wyoming is a beggar state. It cannot balance its own budget, as the state constitution requires, without adding to the national debt. Wyoming's hand is always out for those federal dollars even as our politicians at every level rail against federal spending. Nearly one of every five dollars the state legislature spends comes from the federal government. You'd think a "thank you" would be in order. But, nary a Wyoming politician ever lost a vote carping about the feds. The only federal dollars I've ever seen the state turn down were some of those that would have helped low-income families live a better life. Oddly, it seems as though even those families either don't vote or vote for the politicians who could care less about them and their children.

Today there are nearly as many eligible voters who are not registered to vote than there are those who are registered. A majority of young voting age folks in Wyoming want nothing to do with the democratic process. Unfortunately, that serves the interests of those who have what they need and don't care much about whether anyone else shares. That's why Wyoming has the largest gender wag gap in the United States. Wyoming women are paid about 64 cents for every dollar in wages paid to their male counterparts. The national average is 80 cents. A *Fortune* magazine writer estimates it will be at least 2153 to catch up.[157] It's a good thing we live in "the Equality State." Otherwise it might take another century.

The wage gap worsens for Wyoming's more vulnerable populations, e.g. Native Americans and other women of color as well as women over 55 years of age. It means that more than half of the single mothers in our state are raising children in poverty though they work full time, some working multiple, no-benefit jobs. I largely avoided the disparity by working for the state and federal government but I still remember how humiliating it was for my mother when she was confronted with this sort of job-based discrimination, which was as much or more about her physical disability as it was her gender. She was an accomplished tailor and seamstress, having worked for many years in that profession before coming to Cheyenne. When she applied for a job at a Cheyenne tailor's shop, she was told she would be paid half the normal salary because of her hearing impairment.

Another reason for the wage gap is the heartless way in which Wyoming implemented a welfare reform measure that was enacted by Congress more than two decades ago. President Bill Clinton said the reforms would "end welfare as we know it." He also promised that as people were forced off the welfare rolls, they would find jobs that paid a livable wage. Wyoming cared only about reducing the welfare rolls. It never planned to offer livable wages.

The state received countless accolades for forcing more people, per capita, from welfare than any other state in the Union. Many of these people were struggling single mothers. I always thought it hypocritical that lawmakers and voters who rambled on about how mothers belonged in the home raising their children exhibited no remorse about forcing poor mothers to leave their children at home and go to work. Most often, these mothers were then as they are today, unable to find affordable child care.

After welfare reform, these moms and low-income men became a forced labor supply for employers who could not or would not pay wages that would allow parents to put food on the table and care for their families. Nearly all of these inadequate jobs failed to provide health insurance.

As a result, most of these families made so little in wages that they qualified for food stamps and healthcare under Medicaid. They have to work full time for nearly half a month to afford the rent on a one-bedroom apartment. What did Wyoming's legislators do about this? They refused to raise the minimum wage to a level that would allow these folks to leave public benefit programs and then launched a tirade of abuse toward these families claiming they were lazy. Well, there is nothing harder than being poor. I learned that watching my mother and father try to buy groceries and pay the rent when the Union Pacific paid little to their miners while jacking up prices in the company store. I've been where these families are and have experienced the life their children live.

It's why I have devoted time and money to support scholarships at the University of Wyoming and Laramie County Community College. Any of the successes I have enjoyed in the course of my life are rooted in the excellent education I received first in Rock Springs and later at the University of Wyoming. I never forgot the sacrifice my parents, themselves deprived of the opportunity, made in order that I might have the opportunity. It was they who instilled a solid work ethic in me. Not everyone has had the same upbringing and, therefore, the same opportunities in life. I came to know that it is support from others, including those you may never meet, that makes it possible for all of us. Nobody does it on their own. I have deep philosophical disagreements with friends who believe we all have an equal opportunity. My parents didn't and neither do thousands of other youngsters in Wyoming.

It's like a game of musical chairs. We played that game as kids. The setup is that there are always fewer chairs than players. The music starts to play. The children circle the chairs, walking slowly, anticipating when the music will stop. When it does, they all dive for a vacant chair. But someone gets left out, loses, and departs the game.

Life is like that. The music starts when we are conceived but there are never enough chairs around the circle for everyone. The music inevitably stops. For some it is at birth. Perhaps they are born with physical or mental limitations. Perhaps they are born into families unable to meet their needs. Maybe the music stops later as they experience the ups and downs of life. But it will stop and when it does, there are never enough chairs for everyone to remain in the game.

My financial support for the University in Laramie and the Community College in Laramie County is intended to place a few more chairs around the circle. I write those checks thinking about my parents. It's my hope that some child who may not otherwise be able to get an education, will walk across that stage as I did and be handed a diploma, the key to a better future not only for them but for their children as well.

While I am proud that I have the financial capacity to support students, I have often been disappointed with the administrators at the University of Wyoming. It started with the Black 14 incident for which the University never had the decency to apologize. But, in recent years, the University has had a propensity to listen to powerful legislators with ties to the mining industry more than to the general public. I suppose that is to be expected in a state with only one four-year school dependent on the legislature for its funding. Yet, it seems to me that is good cause to be more courageous, especially in matters of academic freedom.

WHAT KIND OF CRAP IS THIS?

The *Carbon Sink* incident still sticks in my craw. In July 2011, Chris Drury, a British artist, made plans to create a unique sculpture on the UW campus. Drury was well-known for employing the natural environment to make artistic statements. In this case, he crafted a message about the relationship between Wyoming's powerful oil and gas colonizers to international climate change. Mr. Drury used beetle-kill timber interspersed with coal in a vortex shape, placing the work of art in the middle of the UW campus.

Scientists attributed climate change as the cause of the death of millions of trees in the Rocky Mountains as a result of beetles burrowing into their trunks. "Warmer winters allow the pine beetle to thrive and, as a direct consequence, vast tracts of forests in the Rockies are dying," UW's news release quoted Chris Drury. "So, I am about to make a large and very black work on campus, using coal and charred tree trunks in the shape of a whirlpool spiraling down into the earth."

Carbon Sink was intended to create a conversation about Wyoming's contribution to the problem. The UW administrators who approved the sculpture wrongfully assumed they had the authority to do so. They learned differently in short order. In addition to creating a work of art, Mr. Drury created a well-orchestrated storm starting with the mining industry, blowing through legislators who serve at their pleasure, and into the office of the President of the University.

Artist Drury's blog said, "By day three of construction, the mining industry was accusing the university of ingratitude towards one of its main benefactors in what some have seen as a veiled threat to cut funding."

"What kind of crap is this," Wyoming Mining Association director Marion Lummis screamed via an email to UW's vice-president for government affairs Don Richards. As though the industry had been making voluntary, charitable contributions to the University, Loomis then told reporters, "They get millions of dollars in royalties from oil, gas, and coal to run the university, and then they put up a monument attacking me, demonizing the industry."

Before anyone could see the sculpture, the mining industry began bullying Tom Buchanan, the University's president. They enlisted a group of always-useful and powerful legislators. The GOP House Majority Leader and later Speaker was first. Public records demonstrate Rep. Tom Lubnau's threats included cutting the school's funding and even sanctioning a second four-year institution to compete with UW. "I read with amazement," he wrote Buchanan, "the choice of sculpture for the University of Wyoming campus." Lubnau continued, "I am considering introducing legislation to avoid any hypocrisy at UW by insuring that no fossil fuel derived tax dollars find their way into the University of Wyoming funding stream." The GOP legislator then emailed Republican colleagues accusing UW of "biting the hand that feeds" and encouraging them to support the creation of a competing school if UW doesn't get the message.

Then came Kermit Brown, a legislator representing Albany County, UW's home. Rep. Brown was then chair of the House Judiciary Committee and in line to become Speaker. He continued the attack. "This sculpture almost seems to mandate that we have a second four-year school in this state open to the interest of those who make the state successful," said Brown. He wasn't talking about the faculty and students at the school or the families like mine who struggled and sacrificed so that their children could get a UW education. He was, of course, speaking about the hotshots running the mines and taking Wyoming's wealth elsewhere with little concern about the environmental wreckage they were leaving for the next generation. Rep. Brown then threatened the UW president. "We are going to get to the bottom of who knew what and when they knew it."

Initially President Buchanan defended the idea of academic freedom but soon his spine dissolved as the threat mounted and large donors like Peabody Coal announced its two-million-dollar gift to the school was on the line.

One morning as students and faculty arrived on campus, they found that overnight *Carbon Sink* had ceased to exist. There one day, all that was left the next was a patch of newly planted sod. Initially the school President feigned a lack of knowledge about its disappearance. However, a public records request exposed his email to UW Art Museum Director Susan Moldenhauer. "Given the controversy that it has generated, it would be best for UW if the fire pit ("I've forgotten the name of the work") could be removed post haste.

Carbon Sink was destroyed in a rather artful way if you believe art should send a message. An email to Buchanan assured him it was gone. "Some of the larger logs were kept in our bone yard, the smaller ones were dispersed. The coal was taken to our Central Energy Plant and used in the boilers to produce heat." It was ashes to ashes, carbon to the atmosphere. And so, *Carbon Sink* was gone and with it much of the credibility of the school with folks like me who believe an institution of higher learning should be a place willing to engage controversy.

As though the mining companies didn't already have enough influence on the University's agenda, the legislature voted to change the manner in which trustees can be appointed. It has always been the case that board membership was divided between the two political parties. Only seven members of one party could serve at any one time on the UW board. That changed in 2016. Now the Republican Party is permitted by law to hold nine of the 12 seats.

OH WYOMING. THAT'S WHERE THEY KILLED THAT GAY KID

In early October of 1998, I was on a bus tour of New England, enjoying that wonderful time of the year in that part of the country. It was what Robert Frost called a "hushed October morning mild" as I waited to board the bus. I walked to the desk of the hotel and bought the day's *New York Times.* There on the front page was a horrifying story of a young man who had been found hanging from a fence in the Medicine Bow National Forest outside of Laramie, Wyoming. The first responder reported the face of the slight young man was covered in blood with the exception of the place where his tears had carved a track from his eyes to his chin.

That is the way the world was introduced to Matthew Shepard.

His story unfolded dramatically as he lingered for some hours before he died. As the facts developed, we learned he had been beaten with the butt end of a .357 Magnum hand gun by two young men Matthew's age. They had befriended him at a Laramie bar earlier that evening, decided to rob him, lured him to come with them, drove to the remote forest and killed Matthew. After beating him, the two tied Matthew to the fence with clothesline, took his wallet from Matthew's back pocket, and drove away. Matthew hung on that fence bleeding for as long as 18 hours before being discovered by a passing mountain biker. He was taken to a hospital in Ft. Collins, Colorado, where he remained in a coma until he died four days later.

The two young men who were responsible for Matthew's death were convicted and are still doing penance at the Wyoming State Penitentiary. However, Wyoming has never come to grips with the extent to which its image around the nation was impacted by the murder.

From the moment I read the front-page story in the *New York Times,* and the world heard about the case in their newspapers, on television, and radio, everything about the case drew intense national coverage. We all waited along with Matthew's parents, hoping to hear positive reports from the hospital. Matthew's funeral drew media from around the world. The memorial service in Casper was broadcast on public radio. Mourners from around the country, including emissaries sent by President Bill Clinton, filled the church to overflowing. Hundreds of other mourners stood outside in the snow singing "Amazing Grace." Those awful people from the so-called Westboro Baptist Church in Kansas came to use this boy's funeral as a platform to spew hate at gays. However, those who loved Matthew were prepared. Using sheets and wooden poles they constructed angel wings and held them up to block any view of the thugs from Westboro.

For years after the tragedy, when I was introduced to strangers around the nation, the first thing they'd say is something like, "Oh Wyoming. That's where they killed that gay kid." That image may have diminished in the two decades since "they killed that gay kid," but the anti-gay sentiments that gave permission to the killers to take Matthew's life have not.

In the wake of the horrific event, the President and members of Congress called on lawmakers to pass laws creating enhanced criminal penalties when anyone is targeted because of their race, gender, or sexual orientation. In spite of the fact that Matthew Shepard's murder was the catalyst for these laws, legislators of the so-called Equality State and the legislatures of three deep South states are the ones continuing all these years later refusing to protect the victims of these sorts of crimes. Worse yet was when the Wyoming congressional delegation were in the overwhelming minority when all three opposed the "Shepard-Byrd Hate Crimes Prevention Act."

An editorial in the *Casper Star-Tribune* on the 15th anniversary of Matthew's death, spoke the truth when it said, "There's a long way to go before the gay community feels all the benefits of being equal in the Equality State." Much the same can be said for women as well as racial and religious minorities.

---

157   Annalyn Kurtz, "Here's How Long It Will Take for Each State to Give Women Equal Pay, http://fortune.com/2017/03/22/pay-gap-wyoming-florida-census/ accessed June 7, 2017.

CHAPTER TWELVE

THE MOST INTERESTING MAN IN THE WORLD

Two of the most important people in my life became friends soon after I arrived in Cheyenne from the University of Wyoming. One was Margie O'Brien. The other was Kirk Knox.

I met Margie soon after I arrived in Cheyenne. Margie was a radio personality, well like throughout Cheyenne. She had an enormous following on her KFBC radio program. She liked people and they liked her. As a child, Margie lived in Denver where she danced professionally. She came to Cheyenne a couple of years before I arrived. She promptly began a career in radio and TV. Like most women, Margie was never paid what she was worth given the enormity of her popularity. But she plowed ahead with characteristic determination.

Margie was a trailbreaker for women in journalism, winning many awards for her work. She and her husband Paul moved to Phoenix in 1962 to operate a radio station the couple owned. She returned to Cheyenne in 1970. Later Margie was the President of the Wyoming Press Women and other organizations advocating for the progress of women in broadcasting. Later she made a complete shift. After studying yoga for years, Margie spent many of her last years teaching others.

Margie was a joy. She was one of those friends whose values made you want to be a part of her life. She was bright and accomplished, driven, kind, and always optimistic. Margie died on September 29, 2015.

By the time Kirk Knox died on November 22, 2005, he and I had been close friends for more than half a century. It is not, I think, and overstatement to suggest that Kirk was one of the most extraordinary characters in Wyoming's history. Unlike the handsome man in the Dos Equis beer commercial, Kirk may not have been "the most interesting man in the world," but he'd have been high on the list. Some have called Kirk a Renaissance man and maybe that's a good description. It describes one who is open to the world, curious and interested in everything around him. A renaissance man keeps mind, body, and spirit in good shape. It is someone who is comfortable in their own skin.

There is a Greek word that perhaps more aptly speak to who Kirk was. *Polymathes* literally means "having learned much." A person worthy of the adjective is known for an ability to draw from a variety of reservoirs of knowledge. That was Kirk Knox. He could discuss politics, religion, sports, history, and current events with anyone.

Wyoming was fortunate to have someone of Kirk's abilities though Wyoming was not his first choice. He grew up in Exira, Iowa, where he was born on September 3, 1919. One day, his father came home to announce he had bought a store in LaGrange, Wyoming. The family would be moving west. Kirk was in high school and not at all happy about moving to a place he called "the end of the world." He protested by refusing to go to school at all during their first year in the Southeast Wyoming community. But he eventually relented and made the best of it. He was a star athlete and played the coronet. After his death, I served as the personal representative of his estate. Among his earthly goods was a coronet. I learned it had been made in 1860. Kirk learned to play on that antique and kept it for all of the days of his life, winning a regional music competition in Denver one year.

He is best remembered as a newspaper writer. A reporter named Jim Howard, who landed in Rock Springs after graduating from Notre Dame, introduced me to Kirk in the early 1950s. Kirk had just arrived in Cheyenne where he went to work for the *Wyoming State Tribune*. More than a decade earlier, he had worked for the *Scottsbluff Herald*. Then came Pearl harbor. Kirk enlisted in the U.S. Army. Although Kirk was never able to attend college, his IQ was in the genius range. His abilities were obvious enough that he was assigned to work directly with the Commander of the Seventh Army in Memphis, Tennessee, composing his correspondence, later implementing the new IBM card-based computer system.

The Commander was a big baseball fan and wanted to recruit the best possible Army team. He asked Kirk to use the new computer to search for soldiers who had played baseball. With Kirk's computer skills, the Commander assembled a team that won the Army championship.

During these years, he met a woman and fell deeply in love. She was a newspaper writer who imparted a great deal of her wisdom to Kirk during those years. But he left Memphis when his military career ended with medical problems necessitating his honorable discharge in 1944. He lost contact with the woman but later returned for a visit, disappointed to find she had become a "religious Zealot." Kirk was never much for religion. The return visit helped him put her behind.

By now, Kirk's parents were living in Scottsbluff, Nebraska. After his discharge, he joined them and found work writing for the *Herald* and later as the news editor for KOLT Radio Station. Some years later, he noticed an ad in the Cheyenne newspaper. The *Wyoming State Tribune* needed a reporter. Kirk applied, was hired, and spent most of the rest of his life there.

According to a November 29, 2005, eulogy in the *Wyoming State Tribune,* he was known as 'Mr. News' in Cheyenne. He covered every kind of news story and interviewed the famous, infamous and people of note. He interviewed a myriad of nationally famous people. He met and wrote feature stories about every U.S. president since Roosevelt. Some of the others were Ted and Robert Kennedy, Barbara Stanwyck, Bobby Darin, Louis Armstrong, Tip O'Neill, Gary Hart, Casey Tibbs and George Plimpton. Some of the nationally known trials he wrote about where those of Charles Starkweather, Richard and Deborah Jahnke, Mark Hopkinson and Kim Pring. He periodically wrote freelance pieces for newspapers that refused to hire him because he didn't have a college degree, publications like the New York Times, CBS, NBC, Newsweek, Christian Science Monitor, *TIME* magazine and the *Denver Post.* In addition, he occasionally reported on local radio stations and appeared on Cheyenne's TV station newscasts.

Whenever he interviewed a subject for the paper, he took careful notes verbatim. I didn't know of any time anyone ever accused him of misquoting. Kirk steadfastly refused to align himself with any political party or candidate and maintained a reputation as an honest, fair reporter.

Kirk and I spent a great deal of time together. We went to concerts and plays, sports and cultural events. He was an accomplished tennis player. He once played tennis with George Plimpton, a writer whose thing was what he called "participatory sports writing." He pitched an exhibition game between American and National League teams managed by Mickey Mantle and Willie mays. He sparred three rounds each with boxing greats Archie Moore and Sugar Ray Robinson, living to write about it in *Sports Illustrated*. One day, Plimpton was in Cheyenne to speak. Kirk called him at his motel room and talked him into playing a couple of sets of tennis.

Lois and Kirk Knox between sets in a game of tennis.

I had tried the game in high school back in Rock Springs, but hadn't acquired a love of the game or much talent at it. That changed when I met Kirk. He taught me to play and gifted me a love of the game. I played often for much of my adulthood, winning tournaments around the state and region.

Kirk never married, though he fell in love a few times. But, his greatest love was animals, dogs in particular, mainly German Shorthairs. One had only three legs but was a trusted companion and pheasant hunting partner. He slept with Kirk, waking him in the morning kicking Kirk's back gently with the one good foreleg he had. Kirk gifted one million dollars of his estate to the Cheyenne Animal Shelter.

A woman friend once asked me why Kirk and I never married. I was offended by the question. "How dare you ask me such a personal question," I shot back. I'd respond the same way today if asked the same question.

EPILOGUE

My beloved mother, Cecelia died on December 28, 1991. I had spent several years caring for her in my Cheyenne home. By now I had retired from my second career, this one at the Wyoming Department of Education. I volunteered my time to the Wyoming office of the American Association of Retired Persons. AARP needed someone who could help write and edit the newsletter with which they communicate with their thousands of Wyoming members. It was a skill I had and so I raised my hand and took on the job. I accepted the chairmanship of the Laramie County Historical Society and spent seven years in that role.

Now, in the winter of my days on this earth, I feel compelled to share my thoughts. You see, I watched my parents and grandparents live on the margins of Wyoming's culture. As poor, working people, my father and my grandfathers' labor was subject to the exploitation of those mining companies that cared a great deal more for the coal that was brought out of the ground than the men who brought it out. They paid low, sporadic wages, sought to destroy the unions that provided protection for the workers, established company stores that sold low quality food for inflated prices, and kept control of the workers and their families by placing them in substandard, company-provided housing in remote places like Winton.

I saw the way in which employers took advantage of my mother's hearing disability. While she was as good a seamstress as they could find, they paid her less than they were required to pay others because of a disability that in no way limited her ability to do the job.

As an honor graduate from the University of Wyoming, holding one of the first accounting certificates issued to a woman in Wyoming history, I ran into the glass ceiling that often kept women down in this state and still determines that they are not paid equal wages. Throughout my professional life, I watched women and people of color struggle for dignity in Wyoming.

I am glad I was given time on this earth to write about my feelings and to advocate for my state to truly become the Equality State. It is such a lofty motto. If lawmakers, policymakers, and decision-makers in government, business, academia, the faith and non-profit communities would only reflect honestly on the lives of those this state leaves behind, it seems they would be compelled by their inherent goodness to make the necessary reforms. Alas, most are bereft of the sort of introspective skills required.

While Rodger McDaniel and I have been engaged in writing this memoir, the gender wage gap has worsened. That seems to be low-hanging fruit. At least conceptually, everyone seems to agree that people who do similar work ought to be paid similar wages. However, getting beyond the rhetoric seems to be an impossible task. The World Economic Forum reported in 2017, that the United States couldn't even rise to the top 40 of all nations on earth in bridging the gap between what men are paid and women earn. Of the 144 nations reviewed, the U.S. ranks 45th, a drop from its previous perch at number 28.[158] Comparing the 50 states, Wyoming was dead last. How can that be ignored in the Equality State? Perhaps it's because there are too few women in the state legislature and other positions where those who care have the opportunity, but currently not the inclination, to do something meaningful to improve that dismal showing.

The inequality of the Equality State makes appearance in a variety of ways, some subtle and others not. For example, the Wyoming Department of Education recently ended a federally funded program that is critical to leveling the playing field for the children of migrant farm workers in the state.[159]

It's not as though the Department of Education officials are unaware of the plight of these students, mostly children of color. Their parents are required to move from state to state for work. The children are in one school for a time and then off to another. These kids need additional assistance in order to stay in school. Many don't. Fewer than half of the children of migrant workers graduate.

The Department of Education, my old employer, is supposed to care. It is supposed to care especially for under served children like these. And for 40 years, they did.

For that time, the Department took federal dollars to develop and operate a program specifically serving this vulnerable group. But, suddenly and without any input from the parents or the public, the Department abruptly ended the program. It cannot escape notice that the decision by the Republican-led agency, comes during times when President Donald trump is engaging the GOP chorus in a well-orchestrated attack on immigrants of color. Still, the callousness with which the Department of Education terminated its responsibility to this particular group of young people is further evidence that the Equality State is not.

YOU'RE THINKING OF WYOMING

Then there are the continuing attacks on the rights of gays, lesbians, bisexual and transgender citizens of Wyoming. Not a session of the legislature goes by that members don't introduce legislation targeting these folks. It's true that many proposals are not enacted, however, simply introducing the bills allows lawmakers and the bigots among their following to engage is hateful speech about that community.

An African-American legislator said that the LGBTQ community was "attempting to carpet-bag" on the civil rights blacks achieved. She said aloud that if the law protected gays and lesbians, we might as well add redheads and short people to the protected list. Another Wyoming lawmaker said that protecting the rights of gays would increase healthcare costs because of the "unique diseases" they carry. A right-wing lobbying group called WyWatch has since folded its tent but once portrayed the struggle against LGBTQ rights as a battle against Satan.

And then there is the continuing stain from the murder of Matthew Shepard. For many outside the boundaries of Wyoming, that incident defines our state. As this book was being finished, a movie entitled "Three Billboards Outside Ebbing, Missouri" was released. By the time you read these words, the film has likely received numerous awards. There is a scene filmed in a bar. Two men are playing pool when they are interrupted by a local law enforcement officer, a hateful bigot determined to make life tougher for anyone in his path. He starts taunting one of the men, telling him he should move to Cuba because they kill gays there.

The young man tells the officer he is mistaken about Cuba. "You're thinking of Wyoming." It's been almost two decades since Matthew Shepard died and still the stain remains.

Most of America, other than the state where he was executed, reacted to Matthew Shepard's murder by enacting hate crimes laws. These are laws that impose enhanced criminal penalties on those who do intentional harm to another based on their sexual identity or orientation. Two decades after Matthew Shepard's horrible death, the state where he died hung on that fence, is one of only four states refusing to enact any sort of hate crimes legislation. Some states, mostly in Plains and Southern states passed hate crime laws but pointedly excluded the LGBTQ community from protection. But it is a travesty that the state takes pride in having no hate protection for anyone and for being among the last to withhold these protections from the LGBTQ community despite evidence that they are in the crosshairs of those who seek to do harm because of how God made others. Likewise, Wyoming steadfastly refuses to enact a non-discrimination law.

Lawmakers in the Equality State are okay with the fact that gays, lesbians, bisexual, and transgender citizens can be summarily fired and lose their livelihoods because of sexual orientation or identity. The Williams Institute at the University of California at Los Angeles calculates this failure leaves more than 15,000 Wyoming citizens at risk of losing their livelihoods to discrimination.[160] It's not for a lack of effort. For a quarter of a century, LGBTQ advocates have attempted to persuade state and local governments to adopt non-discrimination laws. Only Jackson and Laramie have done so and the state legislature has considered, albeit so far unsuccessfully, laws to ban local governments from affording such protections to their people.

Many legislators intentionally put their heads in the sand and from that vantage point claim such a law to be unnecessary. They announce they have never heard of any of their constituents who have actually suffered discrimination so why pass a law. To the contrary, says the UCLA report. Twenty-nine percent of the Wyoming folks who responded to their survey said they had experienced discrimination in their workplaces. One in five had been terminate because of their sexual status and 17% had been turned away from renting a place to live for that reason.

Those numbers not only validate the need for a non-discrimination law, but they expose the dark underbelly of the Equality State. But it's not only LGBTQ issues that bring out the worse in Wyoming politicians. Take the comments of State Representative Gerald Gay. In opposition to doing anything about the gender-wage gap, he said it was simply a matter of "dependability." Men are and women aren't. Representative Gay said that women tend to take every sick day that's available to them, and that's a gender thing." Weeks before he was defeated for re-election, he proudly claimed, "There's a dependability issue about whether they're going to show up for things."[161]

Yes, he was defeated but his attitude about what it means to be the Equality State has not been. Representative Gay, who once complained about being called "gay," was also the legislator who sponsored legislation banning the use of "Sharia law" in the state. It was little more than a gratuitous shot at the small Muslim population in Wyoming at a time when anti-Muslim tensions were high and this politician wanted to take advantage of that circumstance. Because Matt Mead, a moderate Republican Governor, fears the right-wing of his party, Wyoming is still the only state in the Union to refuse to enter into an agreement with the federal government to facilitate the relocation of refugees. Expressing bigotry-conflated conspiracy theories espoused by much of the far right, Republican State Representative Marti Halverson said she opposes such an agreement until certain questions are answered to her satisfaction. This public official, elected by the voters who apparently share her views, wanted to make sure that any refugees entering the Equality State were the "right kind of persons" regardless of what sort of violence they were fleeing. Halverson asked:

> *"Can Wyoming residents ask that a plan accepts refugees from some country and not others? Or, of some race and not another? Of some sexual preference and not another?"*[162]

Refugees are people fleeing their homeland because of violence and threats to their lives. They have to prove that their lives and/or the lives of their children are at serious and immediate risk if they return to their homeland. Even Mississippi and Alabama understand that and have agreed to relocate people at such risk. But, not the so-called Equality State.

As the writing of this book concludes, there are other politicians promoting the construction of a Heart-Mountain-like prison camp for detained deportees in Evanston. The U.S Immigration and Customs Enforcement officials would like a private, for-profit prison to be isolated from too much public scrutiny where they can indefinitely detain hundreds of people awaiting judicial determination about whether they will be deported. Evanston, Wyoming fits the bill. While you might have thought Wyoming had learned its lesson with the Heart Mountain experience, the state is still run by those who would sell their soul for a few jobs and an up-tick in tax revenues. There are those who believe Wyoming is better than this, but they remain a minority. So, while it may be good politics, it is certainly not equality. It seems that policymakers and decision makers throughout the state seize the day for any opportunity to deny that Wyoming is the Equality State. Carpe diem, Wyoming.

Wyoming adopted its motto honorably at a time when it had actually earned it. And, yet today the state proudly teaches youngsters of the time when Wyoming was the first to give women the right to vote, allowed the first woman to serve on a jury and hold a judgeship for the first time, and, of course, that time when we elected the first female governor in the history of the United States. That is what it meant to be the Equality State. But the last of those worthy events happened in 1925, more than nine long decades ago. "We started out pretty good, but we've been losing ground ever since," said Bernadine Craft, one of the last woman to serve in the 30-member Wyoming Senate.

Early in this memoir, I quoted Soren Kierkegaard to the effect that Wyoming can be seen as an illusion within a delusion. I close with another of his quotes. "Life," he said, "must be understood backwards but it must be lived forward." Wyoming needs to be honest about where it has been to know where it should go.

What it means to be the Equality State has changed. The goal line has been moved. A state that did something important for women more than a century ago and elected the first female governor nine decades ago cannot claim to be an equality state unless it continues to value equality in a contemporary context. I am almost 90 and won't see the state earn the motto again but I hope the generation of young women and men who have chosen to live here will. This book opened with a reminder of how a group of Wyoming's best historians found that the most important stories of the 20th century revolved mostly around how poorly women and Native Americans were treated in our state. Let it be that when historians review the 21st century, they will find the top stories to be about how Wyoming regained the integrity behind the motto.

That is why I wrote this memoir and that's why I appreciate it that you have taken some time from your life to read it.

---

158 Richie Bernardo, "2017's Best & Worst States for Women's Equality," Aug 22, 2017, *https://wallethub.com/edu/best-and-worst-states-for-women-equality/5835/*, *accessed November 10, 2017.*

159 Tennessee Watson, "Wyoming Ends Program Supporting Migrant Students," September 18, 2017, http://wyomingpublicmedia.org/post/wyoming-ends-program-supporting-migrant-students, accessed September 18, 2017.

160   Maggie Mullen, "LGBT People in Wyoming Still Lack Protections, Study Finds,"
September 25, 2017, http://wyomingpublicmedia.org/post/lgbt-people-wyoming-
still-lack-protections-study-find, accessed November 9, 2017.

161   Elizabeth Koh, "Wyoming lawmaker says women earn less because they're less
reliable," September 16, 2016, http://www.charlotteobserver.com/news/politics-
government/article102179772.html, accessed November 10, 2017.

162   Julie Fustanio King, "*No Refuge in Wyoming,*" March 18, 2014, http://planetjh.
com/2014/03/18/no-refuge-in-wyoming/ accessed November 30, 2017.

www.ingramcontent.com/pod-product-compliance
Lightning Source LLC
Chambersburg PA
CBHW071220090426
42736CB00014B/2908